P9-BZF-078

SECOND EDITION

THE VIOLENCE OF HATE

Confronting Racism, Anti-Semitism, and Other Forms of Bigotry

JACK LEVIN

Director, The Brudnick Center on Violence and Conflict

Northeastern University

PEARSON

Boston   New York   San Francisco
Mexico City   Montreal   Toronto   London   Madrid   Munich   Paris
Hong Kong   Singapore   Tokyo   Cape Town   Sydney

Senior Series Editor: *Jeff Lasser*
Series Editorial Assistant: *Erikka Adams*
Senior Marketing Manager: *Laura Lee Manley*
Production Administrator: *Claudine Bellanton*
Editorial-Production Service: *WestWords, Inc.*
Text Design/Electronic Composition: *WestWords, Inc.*
Composition Buyer: *Linda Cox*
Manufacturing Buyer: *Debbie Rossi*
Cover Administrator: *Elena Sidorova*

For related titles and support materials, visit our online catalog at
www.ablongman.com.

Between the time website information is gathered and then published, it is not
unusual for some sites to have closed. Also, the transcription of URLs can result
in typographical errors. The publisher would appreciate notification where these
errors occur so that they may be corrected in subsequent editions.

Library of Congress Cataloging-in-Publication Data

Levin, Jack
   The violence of hate: confronting racism, anti-semitism, and other
   forms of bigotry/ Jack Levin. — 2nd ed.
       p. cm.
   Includes bibliographical references and index.
   ISBN 0-205-46087-9
   1. Hate crimes. 2. Racism 3. Antisemitism. 4. Toleration. I. Title
   HV6773.5.L48 2007
   305.8—dc22   2006043010

Printed in the United States of America

10   9   8   7   6   5   4   3   2   1   11   10   09   08   07   06

To the memory of Irving S. Brudnick

CONTENTS

PREFACE

Etched permanently into my consciousness, two childhood memories caused me to recognize early in life that many of the apparently unique experiences of victimized groups actually have much in common. First, I recall hearing my mother recount the stories of her family's threatened existence in 1930s Frankfort, Germany, and her harrowing escape from her Nazi tormentors. Thanks in large part to the incredible farsightedness of my grandfather, she narrowly avoided being sent to a death camp and fled from Germany when it was still possible to do so. Not for one moment after finally arriving in the United States did she take for granted the privileges of citizenship in her host country. Second, I grew up in the South during the final days of Jim Crow segregation, at a time when Black Americans were still forced to ride in the back of the bus, to use "colored" restrooms and water fountains, and to take only the dirtiest and lowest-paying jobs. Although I never personally witnessed anyone being murdered because of skin color, I did see Black Americans exploited and humiliated on an everyday basis. Hitler was *Der Fuhrer*, but the ideas that Hitler espoused transcend time and national boundaries.

The second edition of *The Violence of Hate* emphasizes the commonalities joining rather than the differences separating those in society who have been victimized because they are different in terms of their race or religion. It explores under a single conceptual framework two important yet perplexing forms of hate and prejudice: racism in American society and the historical occurrence of anti-Semitism with special emphasis on Nazi Germany. Moreover, to provide a broad comparative perspective, the experiences of other groups (for example, Armenians massacred in 1915, renegade Christians acting as servants of power, and gay students victimized by violence) have been introduced at relevant points throughout the book.

This revision of the book has given me a much needed opportunity to update my ideas and examples. Since completing the first edition during the summer of 2001, incredibly important changes in society have occurred. In the aftermath of the September 11, 2001 terrorist attack and the continuing conflicts in the Middle East, the treatment of American Muslims has turned decidedly negative. Over the same period, a "new anti-Semitism" has developed in which Jews around the world are being held responsible for Israeli government policies.

I take the position that support for both racism and anti-Semitism originates not in the ranting and raving of bigoted extremists at the margins of society but in the tacit approval of ordinary, even decent, people who are located squarely in the mainstream. Relatively few Americans actively dabble in bigotry, and even fewer are hardened hatemongers. But millions of individuals who would not dream of committing a hate crime nevertheless contribute to the cause of prejudice by sympathizing with those who do perpetrate hate attacks. In addition, there are countless numbers of otherwise virtuous people in society who remain passive spectators to bigotry because they benefit in either a psychological or socioeconomic sense from the status quo. Although lacking in virulent prejudice, these spectators also lack the courage required to pay the price for doing the right thing. For many, spectatorship is all too comfortable.

Some observers have suggested that racism and anti-Semitism have declined to the point where they no longer threaten the well-being of society's members. From this viewpoint, although prejudice has become harmless or benign, certain environmental or genetic characteristics of marginalized groups continue to play an important role in maintaining group inequalities.

Rejecting this view, I argue that hate is alive, well, and living in our communities where it continues to have a major impact on the access to opportunities and personal safety of millions of Americans. Depending on the circumstances at a particular point in history, hate can remain latent and concealed, making its presence felt in only the most subtle or even unconscious ways until such time that a particular religious or racial group becomes a challenge or threat. Moreover, even where hate and prejudice have declined, it takes relatively few hate incidents to escalate a situation into large-scale intergroup conflict.

Unlike those who assert that hate is a result of either culture or self-interest, I suggest that it is a consequence of both. Hate is normal, expected, and, in many cases, quite rational. Respect for differences can be so costly in a psychological and material sense that it may actually require rebellious or deviant behavior. In a final chapter, I suggest strategies for producing rebels, deviants, and other decent people.

Speaking of decent people, I take this opportunity to thank a number of my colleagues, students, and family members who have unselfishly donated their ideas, criticisms, and suggestions for improving the form and substance of this book. In particular, I am grateful to Kayleen U. Oka, former Director of Multicultural Services at Edmonds College, and Stephen L. Wessler, Director of the Center for the Prevention of Hate Violence, whose insights and recommendations have been liberally sprinkled throughout my work. I am indebted to the following colleagues who have influenced my thinking about the origins of racism and anti-Semitism: Arnie Arluke, Chip Berlet, Randy Blazak, Kathleen Blee, Barry Bluestone,

William Brustein, Richard Cole, Ed Dunbar, Howard Ehrlich, Amitai Etzioni, Raphael Ezekiel, Luis Falcon, Jamie Fox, Meridith Gould, Bob Hall, David Hall, Mark Hamm, Will Holton, Matt Hunt, Range Hutson, Paul Iganski, Valerie Jenness, Billy Johnston, Tony Jones, Debbie Kaufman, Nancy Kaufman, Tom Koenig, Harlan Lane, Richard Lapchick, Fred Lawrence, Yueh-Ting Lee, David Lennox, Brian Levin (no relation), Larry Lowenthal, Jack McDevitt, Karen McLaughlin, Bill Miles, Petar-Emil Mitev, Marvin Nathan, Vincent Parillo, Monte Paulsen, Mark Potok, Emmett Price, Michel Prum, Gordana Rabrenovic, Debbie Ramirez, Tom Shapiro, Michael Sutton, Andy Tarsy, Robert Treston, Evelyn Umlas, Geoff Ward, Joe Warren, Meredith Watts, and Darnell Williams. I am grateful to Scott Wolfman and his outstanding staff at Wolfman Productions: Greg Bura, John O'Marra, and Sarah Rine, for their expert guidance in helping to educate generations of college students about the tragedy of hate and violence. The following students and former students provided valuable feedback about my ideas concerning prejudice and violence: Spencer Blakeslee, Kevin Borgeson, Candice Botes, Lorenzo Boyd, Christina Braidotti, Katie Conner, Sarah Cope, Tara Doran, Julie Doucette, Vin Ferraro, Janese Free, Stephanie Johnson, David Kay, Colleen Keaney, Megan Krell, Phil Lamy, Bill Levin (no relation), Eric Madfis, Jason Mazaik, Liz Mengers, Daniela Methe, Jeff O'Brien, Nelly Oliver, Liz Ridge, Peter Roby, Jeff Sadowsky, Mike Smith, Ben Steiner, and Stas Vysotsky.

The members of my wonderful family—my wife Flea, our children Michael, Bonnie and Brian Bryson (and now Benjamin), and Andrea and Mike Segal (and now Jaden), as well as my brothers and sisters, Carol Weiner, Linda and Lenny Wolf, and Steffie and Mike Lench—have provided the support and encouragement I needed to move through the stages of a project that demanded both time and energy. I have always appreciated their love, tolerance, and patience.

Finally, I am extremely grateful to Betty Brudnick. She and her late husband Irv (Shim) gave me the inspiration I needed to believe that we can change the world for the better.

Jack Levin

CHAPTER 1

PERSPECTIVES ON HATE AND VIOLENCE

HATE, PREJUDICE, AND DISCRIMINATION

Language becomes modified over time in response to changing events and situations. Until recently, the term "hate" referred to any intense dislike or hostility, whatever its object. In everyday conversation, for example, an individual might be said to "hate" his teacher, the taste of liver, communism, or even himself. Thus, in this generic sense of the term, hate could be directed at almost anything—a person, a group, an idea, some other abstraction, or an inanimate object (Levin and Paulsen, 1999).

Transforming the Terms

Beginning in the mid-1980s, in response to a series of racially inspired murders in New York City, the term "hate" became used in a much more restricted sense to characterize an individual's negative beliefs and feelings about the members of some other group of people because of their race, religious identity, ethnic origin, gender, sexual orientation, age, or disability status (Jenness and Broad, 1997; Jenness and Grattet, 2004; Jacobs and Potter, 1998; Levin, 1992–1993; Levin and McDevitt, 1993; Lawrence, 1999). As incorporated into the concept of *hate crime*, this more limited usage overlaps terms such as "prejudice," "bias," "bigotry," "ethnocentrism," and "ethnoviolence" (as in such more specific forms as racism, sexism, ageism, homophobia, and xenophobia—Perry, 2003).

"Hate" is not the only concept in the lexicon of bigotry to have undergone a major shift in meaning. Very much the same sort of transition occurred decades earlier in the original definition of the kindred term "prejudice"—from "any pre-judgment" to "a hostile attitude directed specifically toward the members of an outgroup" (Erhlich, 1972; Levin and Levin, 1982).

In its original usage, the term "prejudice" was used in a legal context to refer to a prejudgment about the guilt or innocence of a defendant, that is, an evaluation made before all the facts of a case could be properly determined and weighed. This usage was subsequently broadened to

1

include "any unreasonable attitude that is unusually resistant to rational influence" (Rosnow, 1972, p.#53). Thus, a person who was stubbornly committed to a position in the face of overwhelming evidence to the contrary could be characterized as prejudiced, whether about her politics, her religious convictions, her friends, or her children.

After the publication of Gordon Allport's classic work, *The Nature of Prejudice*, in 1954, the term "prejudice" was no longer reserved for characterizing people who jump to conclusions or make dogmatic judgments and instead became associated more narrowly with bigotry, bias, and racism. Thus, a prejudiced individual was someone who stereotyped the members of a particular race as, for example, dirty, lazy, and stupid; despised the people in a particular group for being uncivilized and inferior; or felt sickened by the very thought of those who had a different skin color or religious orientation. The original irrationality was retained in Allport's definition, but he applied it much more narrowly to refer to a negative attitude toward other people because they are in a different race, religion, or ethnic group.

Decades later, the same concept was applied to a wider range of differences including sexual orientation, disability status, gender, and age (see Levin and Levin, 1982; Levin and McDevitt, 1995a). At this point, the phenomena of hate and prejudice were, for most purposes, treated as interchangeable.[1]

Prejudice Versus Discrimination

By the same token, Allport considered discrimination prejudice's behavioral counterpart—as hurtful, harmful, destructive behavior toward others because they are perceived to be members of a particular group. Violence represents an extreme version of discrimination; but other examples include name-calling, vandalizing, threatening, firing, or refusing to have contact with individuals who are different.

The relationship between hate or prejudice, on the one hand, and discrimination, on the other has been well documented. There is reason to believe that certain hate offenses *result from* some personal bias or hatred. Perpetrators may act out of prejudicial beliefs (i.e., stereotypes)

---

[1]Although overlapping and used interchangeably in this work, "hate" and "prejudice" also have differences that are important to emphasize. "Hate" tends to focus less on cognition (i.e., stereotyping) and more on the emotional or affective component of bigotry. Indeed, until hate became recently associated with intergroup hostility, researchers focused almost exclusively on the cognitive dimension of prejudice. As a result, sociologists and psychologists have offered many more insights into the nature of stereotypes and other cognitive processes related to prejudice than they have into its affective basis (Pettigrew, 1997).

and/or emotions (e.g., envy, fear, or revulsion) concerning people who are different. In the extreme case, a hatemonger may join an organized group in order to devote his entire life to destroying a group of people he considers "inferior."

It is not, however, always necessary for hate to precede the bigoted behavior. In fact, from the literature of social psychology, we know that prejudices often develop or at least become strengthened to justify *previous* discriminatory behavior, including violence (see Levin and Levin, 1988).

This is probably true of hate crimes as well as other forms of discrimination. For example, a White teenager may assault someone who is Latino because his friends expect him to comply, not because *initially* he harbors intense hatred toward his victim. If he views the target of his attack as a flesh-and-blood human being with feelings, friends, and a family, the offender may feel guilty. By accepting a dehumanized image of the victim, however, the perpetrator may actually come to believe that his crime is justified. After all, the rules of civilized society apply only to human beings, not to demons or animals. Similarly, an individual may commit an act of violence against an individual for economic reasons (e.g., because he believes that the presence of Blacks in his neighborhood reduces property values) and subsequently become totally convinced that all Blacks are rapists and murderers. Who would want a rapist living next door?

Part of the way that we come to understand ourselves is not very different from the way that others come to know us. We observe the manner in which we act over a period of time. If we repeatedly participate in hate crimes or other discriminatory behavior, we might very well gradually modify our self-image and our thinking about the groups we attack so as to be consistent with how we behave. Once again, we see the impact of discriminatory behavior on hate and prejudice (Bem, 1970).

Most surprisingly, perhaps, individuals who find comfort in joining an organized hate group may not always be so hate-filled as we might believe, at least not at first. In her research into what motivates women who join white supremacist groups, sociologist Kathleen Blee (2003) discovered that many of her respondents became more hateful *after* joining the movement. Their decision to take membership in a hate group was apparently inspired less by prejudice or hate and more by a desire for community; that is, to remain in good standing with their comrades.

The Role of the Individual

During the 1940s and 1950s, the term "prejudice" provided the basis for countless studies of intergroup tension and hostility. One of the most important theories ever developed in the social sciences, the *authoritarian personality structure* (Adorno et al., 1950), took a psychoanalytic viewpoint that located the roots of bigotry in early childhood. Literally thousands of research projects were initiated to test various aspects of the theory.

Yet during the 1960s and later, ripples from the civil rights movement began to make their way through American society. The concept of prejudice fell out of favor with social scientists as vastly more attention became focused on institutionalized rather than individual racism. To a growing extent, the thinking in social science was that racist attitudes (or at least their public expression) were on the decline and that discrimination was more or less independent of hate (see, for example, Schuman, et al., 1997; Levin and McDevitt, 1995a).

Thus, rather than focus on individual prejudices, researchers during the past few decades understandably turned more of their attention to investigating institutional and structural forms of discrimination: in large businesses, for example, how union seniority rules assure that people of color do not get promoted, even if individual union representatives oppose the prevailing system; in college applications, the manner in which SATs indirectly favor White applicants, whether or not individual admissions officers hold racist attitudes; in real estate transactions, how real estate associations, as a matter of policy, "steer" Black home buyers from White neighborhoods, regardless of the racial biases of particular agents (Pearce, 1979).

Because social scientists have enthusiastically examined such structural issues, they may have been surprised when advocacy groups suggested during the 1980s and 1990s that hate violence was dramatically on the rise. The so-called "new" or "modern" racism had emphasized subtle, sophisticated, symbolic, and institutionalized forms of bigotry; it had all but failed to recognize the possibility that policies and programs directed at tearing down the barriers separating various racial and religious groups might also provoke increasing numbers of hate crimes committed by members of traditionally advantaged groups in society who felt under attack.

It might be surprising that a sociologist would argue for bringing back the individual into our theorizing about intergroup conflict, but that is exactly what I think is important to do. Just as Allport (1954) long ago suggested, the individual is a silent partner, an active agent, and a gatekeeper in any process of social change. It is important, of course, to recognize the influence of structural and cultural sources of bigotry, but it is just as significant to realize that it takes individual action or lack of action to make hate happen. Individuals still make the decisions; they conform or refuse to conform to group standards; and they decide whether to go along with the dictates of legitimate authority. Individuals internalize the cultural hate, and many of them also benefit (or they believe that they benefit) from the maintenance of prejudice and discrimination. Based on both company policy as well as on personal preconceptions, real estate agents decide who sees which houses and who doesn't. Based on both school policy and on personal preference, admissions officers decide who gets into school and who is refused admission. Moreover, though depending on institutionalized practices and policies, the overwhelming majority of hate offenses are committed not by organizations but by individuals. The hate expressed in such crimes is far from indirect or sophisticated or abstract; the discrimination is anything but subtle.

HATE AS A JUSTIFICATION FOR VIOLENCE

Several years ago, when Apartheid was still the reigning system of race relations in the country of South Africa, I happened to run across an Associated Press story in the *Boston Globe* concerning an unfortunate White woman in Johannesburg who was being treated for cancer. Through no fault of her own, she had suffered not only a loss of her physical well-being but also a dramatic loss of her social and economic status.

Under the South African system of Apartheid, there were three racial categories: White, Colored, and Black. Actually, the racial identity of South Africans determined almost entirely the range of opportunities they could expect to enjoy over the course of the life cycle, including whom they were eligible to date and marry, where they were permitted to live, what sorts of jobs they were qualified to take, the mode of transportation they were permitted to use, and the quantity and quality of their formal education. With respect to such advantages, Whites were always on top, Coloreds were in between, and Blacks were at the very bottom.

The cancer-stricken South African woman soon learned—on a deeply personal level—the cold, cruel reality of Apartheid. As an unexpected side effect of the chemotherapy she had taken, her skin color became progressively darker, so much so that her racial identity appeared to be Colored, not White, and she was no longer permitted to ride the Whites' only bus to work every day. In fact, the bus driver, thinking that any of the woman's offspring must share at least some part of their mother's racial identity, also refused to permit her teenage daughter to ride the bus, even though the girl's skin color was that of a White. But getting to work turned out to be the least of the unfortunate woman's problems. As soon as her skin darkened, she was also shunned by her friends, fired by her boss, and deserted by her husband.

It should not be shocking that a change that was only skin-deep severely restricted the woman's social and economic opportunities. Under the South African version of Apartheid, an individual who was identified as Black or Colored was also considered less than a human being. In fact, many South African Whites refused to use the word "people" when referring to those designated as Colored or Black. The dehumanization of

South Africans of color was essential to the perpetuation of Apartheid. It permitted both official policy and informal interaction to exclude millions of residents from being treated according to the rules of civilized society. If Blacks are human beings, they must be handled with decency and respect. If they are subhumans or animals, then they can be enslaved, segregated, brutalized, or even killed with impunity.

Social Construction of Differences

One important lesson we learn from the South African example is that we don't always have 100 percent control over the way we are racially defined by other people. If those who define us have more power and authority than we do, then their definition may be real in its consequences (Thomas and Thomas, 1928). Under such circumstances, theirs— not ours—is the definition that counts, at least in terms of its impact on our economic and social status. It is the definition that determines what bus we are allowed to ride, where we are permitted to live, and which schools we are allowed to attend. We may very well be convinced that we are X; and, psychologically, this may be enough to make us feel very comfortable. Yet, in its ability to influence our status in society, what other people believe us to be may, in a socioeconomic sense, determine that we are Y, not X.

Yet, as a physical marker of differences between groups, even skin color is not always an important criterion for determining our racial identity. In South Africa, for example, visiting Japanese businessmen were officially classified as White, that is, as honorary Caucasians, as a purely practical matter to spare them the humiliating effects of being categorized as non-Whites. There would have been no Japanese businessmen visiting South Africa at all if they had been forced to live the lives of its Colored citizens.

To the extent that it is *socially constructed,* racial identity varies over time and place. In the United States until recently, anyone found to possess even one drop of "Black blood" was considered Black. Thus, as late as the 1980s, an individual whose ancestry included even a single Black relative but who appeared to be White (had blonde hair, fair complexion, and Caucasoid physiognomy [thin lips and nose]) would still be treated, in law and custom, as belonging to the Black race. Under many state laws, even choice of a marriage partner would have been restricted to someone else defined as Black.

In refusing to relinquish its archaic legal racial categories, the state of Louisiana, as late as 1983, became the only remaining state to have a legally sanctioned formula for determining the racial identity of its residents. By this mathematical method, any citizen who had one-thirty-second or less of "Negro blood" was considered to be White under the law (Larson, 2000).

Although such state laws no longer exist, absolute criteria for determining Blackness continue to operate on an informal basis within American culture. Thus, for example, golf great Tiger Woods, who is of mixed ancestry and considers himself multiracial, is often referred to by television and radio commentators as the "great Black golfer." Interestingly, individuals defined as Black in the United States could travel to Puerto Rico or Brazil, where, depending entirely on physical appearance instead of genetics, they might very well be considered White. Or they could visit South Africa, where they would almost definitely be thought of as Colored instead of either Black or White.

Racial identity can, in addition to its impact on self-esteem, have a profound political effect. The federal government allocates some $200 billion every year for employment, mortgage lending, housing, health care services, and educational opportunities based on the representation of various racial and ethnic groups in the Census Bureau enumeration. The 2000 U.S. Census contained 63 racial options. Still, many Americans refused to categorize themselves racially and opted instead for "other." For the first time in 210 years, the Census Bureau no longer required Americans to identify themselves in only one racial category and permitted them to circle more than one category.

In light of the dramatic recent changes in the way that they are seeing themselves and others, the multiracial alternative has become increasingly appealing to Americans. In the 2000 Census, for example, some 6.8 million Americans identified themselves as multiracial. Over the past 30 years, marriages between Blacks and Whites have increased by some 400 percent, and marriages between Asians and Whites have increased by 1000 percent. There are now 1.6 million interracial married couples in the United States, 10 times as many as in 1960 (Southern Poverty Law Center, 2001; American Academy of Child and Adolescent Psychiatry, 2005).

As we have seen in the case of the South African woman whose skin darkened, the implications of being defined as a member of one race over another can be highly significant on a personal level. The same can be said for an individual's religious preference, especially if it becomes regarded as an ascribed, racial, and therefore a permanent status. In their own eyes, for example, former Jews living in Nazi Germany during the 1930s who had converted to Christianity were nothing less than devout Christians. In the eyes of the powerful Nazi regime, however, they were Jewish vermin—subhuman enemies of the state who deserved to be singled out, herded off to death camps, and exterminated.

In the same way, the social construction of gayness has often been applied to victims who are bashed because of their presumed sexual orientation. Just as converted German Christians were singled out for discriminatory treatment by anti-Semites, so straight men have been assaulted by homophobic hatemongers. You don't have to be gay to become a victim of a gay hate bashing. Instead, you only have to look gay, that is, you only have to possess some of the characteristics associated in the minds of perpetrators with being gay. Thus, many straight men on college campuses around the country have been threatened or assaulted essentially because they fit the expectations by being "effeminate" in their gestures or expressions (Levin and McDevitt, 2002).

It has long been recognized that age categories do not exist in nature but are socially determined. Human beings invented the period called childhood and created the stage known as adolescence. In many societies, individuals went straight from infancy to adulthood and to a job working in the fields alongside their older brothers and sisters. Elsewhere, childhood exists but adolescence does not. By a certain age, instead of gradually maturing through a separate and distinct developmental stage, children in such societies go through a rite of passage (e.g., at the age of 12, they are required to kill a lion) that establishes them as adults. Even old age is a construction. In one area of the world, the members of a society are regarded as "old" beginning at 45 or 50; in another, they are regarded as reaching old age at 65 or 70. Aging is a gradual process that begins with birth and ends with death. We divide the life cycle into categories as though they were part of the natural order. But they are not.

In the same way, many group differences are socially constructed rather than fixed in nature. This is not to say that groups are identical to one another in each and every respect. In fact, groups of human beings obviously differ markedly in terms of almost every conceivable attribute, including skin color, physiognomy, language, culture, socioeconomic status, level of education, political clout, and so on. Some of these differences frequently form the basis for conflict between groups (Lee, Jussim, and McCauly, 1995). It's just that human beings decide which differences are socially significant and which differences deserve to be ignored.

When Stereotypes Turn Nasty

Our images of the people in different groups can be molded to fit the occasion for which they are needed, regardless of the way the people in question behave. When the members of another group become too competitive or threatening, they are seen not as industrious and hard-working, but as obsessed workaholics; not as laid-back and mellow, but as lazy; not as courageous, but as bloodthirsty; not as thrifty, but as stingy; not as family oriented, but as clannish; not as assertive, but as aggressive; not as having exceptional athletic ability, but as having all brawn and no brains; not as excelling in math and science, but as having a narrow intellect.

The particular stereotype seems to depend at least somewhat on the forms of discrimination it is meant to encourage or justify. Outsiders who are expected to be submissive and subordinate to the interests of the dominant group are often *infantilized*. Their image is that of children. Yet some stereotypes are more life-threatening than others. Those outsiders who are regarded as posing a threat to the advantaged position of the dominant group may be treated not like children but animals or demons (Levin and Levin, 1982).

The derivation of this notion can be traced back to widespread stereotypic thinking among White colonists in which Africans were regarded as apelike heathens and savages controlled almost completely by their senses rather than by their intellect. Their savage behavior was reflected in "primitive" non-Christian religious beliefs and rituals and in reports of their "uncivilized" cultural practices, including polygamy, infanticide, and ritualistic murder (Smith, 1995).

Although predating slavery, such *dehumanizing* ideas about Blacks were quickly rediscovered by European colonists to justify the institution of slavery within the context of an equalitarian ethos. Instead of dealing with the moral consequences of the forced enslavement of an entire group of people based strictly on physiognomy and skin color, the colonists denied the evil of "the peculiar institution" and instead took the moral high ground. Blacks were not people; they were property. From this point of view, they were not victimized or exploited; they were the beneficiaries of a way of life that would ensure their very survival.

Although certainly belittling and degrading, the negative stereotyping of slaves included more infantilization than dehumanization. Blacks who consented to play the role of loyal and lowly slaves were generally regarded as children who needed the wise counsel and guidance of their White masters to survive. The image was that of Little Black Sambo—the musical but ignorant youngster who didn't have the brains to come in out of the rain.

In the years following the end of the Civil War, the infantilized image of Blacks was transformed into a dehumanized stereotype on the basis of which murder and mayhem could be justified. No longer seen as valuable property, Blacks had to fend for themselves. They were unable to rely on their masters to protect them from other racist Whites. Rather than viewed as children, Blacks were now regarded as animals, lacking in human intelligence or spirituality, that needed to be tamed or killed (Levin and Levin, 1982).

Such negative images are often seen in warfare. The underlying causes of a conflict may be economic, but stereotyping facilitates bloodshed. In Northern Ireland, for example, civil strife seems to have been reinforced by a set of stereotypes of Catholics and Protestants that might be expected to describe racial differences alone; for example, that Catholics have shorter foreheads, larger genitalia, and less space between their eyes than do their Protestant neighbors (Levin, 1997b).

Only the nastiest images of newcomers seem to spread during hard economic times, as the native-born population perceives that their financial position is being eroded. At times, certain prejudices become narrowly targeted. During the 1800s and early 1900s, when they came to the United States and competed for jobs with native-born citizens, Irish American newcomers were stereotyped by political cartoonists of the day as apes and crocodiles (Keen, 1986). During the same period, as soon as they began to compete with native-born landowners and merchants, Italian immigrants settling in New Orleans were widely depicted as dangerous members of organized crime who needed to be controlled (Gambino, 1977).

Chinese immigrants to nineteenth-century America tended to be regarded as "honest," "industrious," and "peaceful" so long as jobs remained plentiful. But when the job market tightened and the Chinese began to seek work in mines, farming, domestic service, and factories, a dramatic shift toward anti-Chinese sentiment emerged. They quickly became stereotyped as "dangerous," "deceitful," "vicious," and "clannish." Whites then accused the Chinese immigrants of undermining the American standard of living (Sung, 1961). In a similar way, the depressions of 1893 and 1907 served to solidify the opposition to immigration from Italy, setting the stage for widespread acceptance of stereotypes depicting Italian Americans as "organ-grinders, paupers, slovenly ignoramuses, and so on" (La Gumina, 1973).

On occasion, racial epithets have been voiced by angry Americans to justify injuring or murdering immigrants. In 1994, in a Massachusetts courtroom, 25-year-old Harold Robert Latour was found guilty of second-degree murder and assault and battery with the intent to intimidate based on race. A year earlier, Latour had beaten to death a 21-year-old Cambodian man, Sam Nang Nhem, his neighbor in a Fall River, Massachusetts housing project. The murder occurred after a family clambake, as Nhem and his friend were walking over to a trash bin to discard some clam shells. Latour shouted, "I'm gonna knock that gook out!" Then he kicked his victim to the ground with his steel-toed Doc Martins (Associated Press, 1994).

I played a role in Latour's trial as an expert witness in the area of hate crimes. My task was to inform the jury as to the historical application of the term "gook" as a racial slur. I told the court that the epithet was used by the Allies during World War II to characterize the Japanese enemy, during the Korean conflict to refer to North Koreans, and during the Vietnam war to refer to North Vietnamese and Vietcong. In the mid-1970s, as large numbers of Asian newcomers arrived in the United States, the term "gook" then became a racial slur to discredit all southeast Asian immigrants. The fact that the defendant had shouted an anti-Asian epithet just prior to beating his Cambodian victim indicated that a hate crime had occurred and may have contributed to lengthening Latour's sentence—a life sentence in Walpole state penitentiary with parole eligibility after 15 years.

War is only one source of dehumanizing racial slurs. Organized hate groups have offered their members the dehumanizing images they need to feel justified in their efforts to eliminate "the other." For example, the official Web site of the white supremacist group Aryan Nations recently defined Jews literally as a terminal illness. According to Pastor Jay Faber of Aryan Nations,

> In this world, the races are the parts of the body, and the jew is cancer. When you go to the doctor for cancer treatment, if he tells you that you have almost killed off the cancer, you would never tell the doctor to stop, you would tell him to kill it all. Cancer = jews. Let's join world wide and rid the world of the disease that has inflicted all of us. (http://www.aryan-nations.org/)

IS HATE ON THE DECLINE?

Many forms of hate have softened significantly since World War II. As determined by large-scale surveys of White racial attitudes from 1942 to 1968, there was a sizable increase in the proportion of White Americans willing to support integration of the public schools. Over the same period of time, the proportion of White Americans who regarded the intelligence of Blacks as equal to that of Whites rose considerably (Bellisfield, 1972–73; Hyman and Sheatsley, 1956, 1964). Data from a series of surveys of the American population in 1964, 1968, and 1970 suggested that White and Black attitudes during this period of time moved closer together on questions of principle and policy (Campbell, 1971).

Into the 1970s, hate and bigotry, although clearly on the decline, nevertheless continued to hold a tight grip on the thinking of many Americans. Selznick and Steinberg (1969), in their interviews with a representative cross section of the national population in 1964, found that 54 percent of their respondents thought that Jews always like to be at the head of things, 52 percent agreed that Jews stick together too much, and 42 percent felt that Jews are more willing than others to use shady practices to get what they want. Moreover, Petroni (1972) found frequent usage of racial stereotypes among White midwestern high-school students who were highly critical of the prejudices of their parents and yet who failed to recognize they had prejudices of their own.

With reference to stereotypes associated with Blacks, Brink and Harris (1964) reported that a substantial proportion of a nationwide cross section of White Americans taken in 1963—in some cases reaching almost 70 percent agreement—were willing to agree that Blacks smell different, have looser morals, want to live off the handout, have less native intelligence, breed crime, and are inferior to Whites. In a 1966 survey, Brink and Harris (1967), again conducting a nationwide study of White Americans, found a softening in some of their negativism toward Blacks but still reported about 50 percent who agreed that Blacks smell different, have looser morals, and want to live off the handout. Campbell's 1968 survey determined that of the Whites living in the 15 cities studied, 67 percent said that Blacks push too fast for what they want, 51 percent opposed laws to prevent racial discrimination in housing, and 33 percent said that if they had small children, they would prefer that their children have only White friends.

At least on an abstract level, hate based on race and religion seems to have plummeted over the past several decades. In 1998, a national poll conducted for the Anti-Defamation League found that the number of Americans holding strong anti-Jewish attitudes—agreeing that Jews have too much power and are more loyal to Israel than to America—had declined to only 12 percent from 20 percent in 1992 and 29 percent in 1964. In survey after survey, moreover, the majority of Americans now claimed to be accepting of racial integration, at least as a matter of principle. For example, only 7 percent of all Americans thought that "Blacks and Whites should go to separate schools." Even stereotyped thinking about race seems to have seriously eroded over time. Merely 4 percent now characterized Blacks as "lazy." (In 1967, that figure was 26 percent; in 1933, it was 75 percent)—(Anti-Defamation League, 2001).

Not unlike trends in racial and religious bigotry, Americans have grown increasingly more tolerant of homosexuality over the past several decades. According to Gallup pollsters, the percentage of Americans believing that gays should be given equal job opportunities increased from 56 percent in 1977 to 74 percent in 1992 and to 88 percent by 2003. The percentage believing that homosexuality is an acceptable alternative lifestyle grew from only 34 percent in 1982 to 38 percent in 1992 and to 50 percent by 1999 (Saad, 2005).

Underestimating Bigotry

At the same time, there are certain negative beliefs and feelings about various groups in American society that seem, over the decades, to have persisted and even increased substantially. Since 1999, the percentage of Americans seeing the gay lifestyle as an acceptable alternative has remained at about 51 percent; 45 percent continue to say it is unacceptable. Moreover, more than half of all Americans consistently tell pollsters that homosexual relationships are morally wrong (Saad, 2005).

Recent scandals involving sexual abuse commited by Catholic priests may have caused some backsliding in the acceptance of gays and lesbians.

Between 2003 and 2005, Gallup reported decreases in the percentage of Americans saying that gays should be hired as clergy (from 56 percent to 49 percent), as elementary school teachers (from 61 percent to 54 percent), and as high school teachers (from 67 percent to 62 percent). Moreover, the recent debate concerning the legality of gay marriage has not resulted in overwhelming public support for marriages between homosexuals. According to Gallup, only 39 percent now say that such marriages should be legally valid. Even support for the legality of gay relations between consenting adults is found in less than a majority of Americans. Little has changed since 1977, when 43 percent supported gay relations being legal. In 2003, support for the legality of homosexual relationships increased to 60 percent but then dropped to only 52 percent by 2005 (Saad, 2005).

In some areas, stereotyped thinking about racial and religious groups has also stalled. In a recent Harris telephone survey of 3000 people commissioned by the National Conference for Community and Justice (2000), it was determined that certain stereotypes continue to be accepted not only by Whites, but also by Americans of color (Asians, Latinos, and Blacks). In response to the statement that Asian Americans are "unscrupulous, crafty, and devious in business," some 27 percent of all White Americans registered their agreement, but so did 46 percent of Latinos and 42 percent of African Americans. In response to the statement that Latinos "lack ambition and the drive to succeed," 20 percent of all White Americans agreed, as well as 35 percent of Asian Americans and 24 percent of African Americans. In response to the statement that African Americans "want to live on welfare," 21 percent of all White Americans agreed, but so did 31% of Asian Americans and 26 percent of Latinos.

These results indicate that hate and prejudice have taken on greater complexity as our society has become increasingly multiracial. To the extent that prejudices are indeed cultural, we shouldn't be surprised that they are shared not only by members of the dominant group but also by minority members.

Moreover, arguing that hate and bigotry may be much more widespread than revealed in the typical study, some researchers have called into question the validity of the transparent questionnaire approach for measuring changes in the acceptance of racist stereotypes. Very few Americans, they argue, now want to be known as racists. Therefore, they are unlikely to be honest in answering questions that could make them out to be bigots. Moreover, many respondents may not even be aware of their own racism. In response to straightforward questions about their attitudes, those who hold racist attitudes may give what they see as socially acceptable responses instead of revealing a truth that may be unacceptable even to them (Wachtel, 2001).

In addition to blatant racism, many individuals apparently hold unconscious biases about such characteristics as race, religion, gender, and sexual orientation. Even highly educated and humane individuals, people who sincerely believe that they are entirely free of prejudice or hate, may be totally unaware that they operate from bias or bigotry. For example, researchers writing in the *New England Journal of Medicine* have reported that physicians were 40 percent less likely to order sophisticated cardiac tests in response to complaints about chest pain when the patients were women rather than men and Black rather than White. Blatant sexism or racism didn't seem to be at the basis of these differences in doctors' recommendations. Instead, they made decisions—in this case, life-and-death decisions—on the basis of strongly held yet unconscious biases about gender and race. According to U.S. Surgeon General David Satcher, this could be one factor in explaining why Blacks are 40 percent more likely than Whites to die from heart disease (White, 1999).

Also in support of the notion that we tend to underestimate the presence of prejudice, social psychologists found that Whites' attitudes toward Blacks were reported as substantially more negative when the White subjects believed they had been hooked into an apparatus that monitored their real feelings and beliefs with total accuracy. In this "bogus pipeline" situation, respondents apparently were more willing to reveal the truth about their racist attitudes than risk being caught in a lie (Sigall and Page, 1971).

Research designed to measure concealed prejudice has relied on making inferences about the respondents' attitudes based on their behavior. In one experiment, for example, White Princeton University students who believed they were participating in a study of interviewing techniques were asked to question, on a random basis, either someone Black or someone White. In comparison with students assigned to a White interviewee, their counterparts with a Black interviewee conveyed more negative nonverbal behavior while interacting. More specifically, they chose to sit farther apart, spent a shorter period of time together, and made a larger number of errors in their speech while talking. Apparently, the White students unwittingly expressed a degree of discomfort based on their unconsciously held feelings and beliefs about Black people (Word, Zanna, and Cooper, 1974); yet, if you had asked them bluntly to express their attitudes toward Blacks, there is every reason to believe that they would have painted a glowing, or at least an unbiased, picture.

Another factor in the underestimate of bigotry is that at least some hate remains unverbalized beneath the surface, even ready to strike. In January 2001, almost two years after he was laid to rest at the age of 81, Richard J. Cotter's racism and anti-Semitism first became publicly apparent. The one-time Massachusetts assistant attorney general and long-time bachelor left $750,000 to organized hate groups—more than $500,000 to a church in Louisiana led by a founding member of the American Nazi Party; $100,000 to Andrew Macdonald, the author of a White supremacist novel entitled *The Turner Diaries;* $25,000 to the Confederation of Polish Freedom Fighters; and $100,000 to a Holocaust denier from Toronto. One of his acquaintances of more than 23 years referred to Cotter as "a good and decent man," someone so decent that he couldn't even bring himself to euthanize his sick horses. Neighbors saw Cotter as an eccentric man who wanted to be left alone in the house in which he had lived for 40 years. But inside the front doors of that home, the Harvard law school graduate exhibited a series of wooden trophies from anti-Semitic organizations naming him as their man of the year and stacks of books discussing the virtues of White pride and right-wing patriotism. Choosing to conceal his racist beliefs from public scrutiny, Cotter had long served as a legal advisor to neo-Nazi groups (Belkin, 2001).

The Difference Between Small and Insignificant

Even if subtle and concealed variations of hate continue to exist, it is heartening that at least it has become somewhat uncomfortable for individuals to express their bigotry openly without fear of reprimand or retaliation. At the cultural level, therefore, some progress toward respect for differences seems to have been made. However, when it comes to concrete government efforts to implement equal treatment by race, there is considerably less support. In fact, public support for government intervention to integrate schools and equal treatment in the use of public accommodations actually declined beginning in the 1980s (Schuman et al., 1997).

For example, support for affirmative action continues to divide along racial lines. In an August 2005 Gallup survey of American adults, 72 percent of Blacks but only 44 percent of Whites reported that they favor affirmative action programs. The explanation for affirmative action support also divides racially. The majority of White Americans (59 percent) but less than one in four Black Americans (23 percent) believes that Blacks in this country have equal job opportunities (Jones, 2005).

The continuing weakness of White support for the implementation of racial integration is indicated by variations in the willingness to participate personally in integrated settings. Very few White Americans object to neighborhood or school integration when it involves only a small number of Blacks. When Blacks promise to become anything like a majority, however, White support dwindles (Schuman et al., 1997).

Lack of support for integrating neighborhoods, workplaces, and schools aids in keeping groups separated on a daily basis. Even worse, there are those Americans who feel so threatened by diversity and difference that they translate their anxiety and anger into criminal behavior. Of course, only a relatively small number of Americans ever go this far.

There are, for example, many millions of crimes committed every year in the United States, some 9000 of which are officially regarded by the Federal Bureau of Investigation (FBI, 2005) to be hate offenses. Considering there are approximately 290 million people in the United States, FBI data suggest that the likelihood is quite small of any given citizen being attacked because of her race, religion, or sexual orientation.

Hate Crimes Are Vastly Under-Reported

Quite clearly, however, the 9000 FBI figure vastly underestimates the actual incidence of hate episodes. It is really the tip of the iceberg, representing only those incidents that rise to the level of criminal offenses and only those crimes officially recognized as motivated by hate and reported by local police departments as such. Under a voluntary reporting system, some 12,711 police jurisdictions in 49 states and the District of Columbia, representing 86.6 percent of the total population, now report. Still, some states have been more cooperative than others: in 2004, the state of Alabama claimed five hate crimes, Mississippi only two (FBI, 2005).

Basing an estimate of the prevalance of hate crimes on victim rather than police reports causes a substantial increase in the number of reported cases. According to the Bureau of Justice Statistics, 191,000 hate crime incidents were reported annually by victims in its National Crime Victimization Survey (Harlow, 2005).

But even the reports by victims may under-represent the actual prevalence of hate offenses. It isn't only law enforcement personnel who are reluctant to report hate attacks. Many victims also prefer not to inform anyone—and especially not law enforcement officials—that they have been victimized. Having grown up where residents were distrustful of the police, some simply do not believe that law enforcement will be on their side. Moreover, immigrants may have come from countries where repressive regimes were as likely as individual hatemongers to commit atrocities against them. They see the police as "the enemy of occupation." For certain groups, American institutions may similarly not be trusted. A recent survey found that almost 80 percent of Shiite Muslims in the United States who were victims of "post 9-11 discrimination" failed to report the incidents to the police (Religion News Service, 2005).

In 2002, my colleague Jack McDevitt surveyed more than 4000 students at public high schools across the state of Massachusetts as to how many of them had been victims of hate crimes—vandalism, assault, assault and battery, harassment, or sexual assault. He determined that 30 percent of the 400 students victimized by a hate offense told no one that they had been attacked. When victims did inform someone, 60 percent told a friend, 29 percent told a family member, and 15 percent told a school employee. Only 3 percent reported their crime to the police (Rosenwald, 2002).

It Takes Only a Few Bad Apples

Aside from the problem of under-reporting, a second difficulty in assessing the impact of hate crimes involves realistically attempting to determine the level of hate incidents that constitutes a menace. Before writing off the threatening influence of a relatively small number of hate offenses, it would be wise to gain some perspective on the relationship of hate to large-scale ethnic conflict. In Northern Ireland where ethnic warfare seemed, until recently, always to be just around the corner, most violent crimes (robbery, murder, assault, and rape) had nothing to do with religious differences. Yet, all it took to start a new round of terrorist bombings was one murder of a police officer; all that was necessary to ignite a new round of violence was a single terrorist act. Moreover, middle-class citizens of Northern Ireland who lived in the suburbs and took care not to voice their political views in public may have felt immune from the hate attacks directed against impoverished and working-class residents in cities like Derry and Belfast. A count of the hate incidents in Northern Ireland over the past couple of decades might have led one *incorrectly* to conclude that ethnic conflict was no longer a problem there, and that Northern Ireland's Protestants and Catholics were living in peace and tranquility, when they were actully engaged in something approaching civil warfare.

Threatening Situations Can Inspire Hate

Just when you are convinced that stereotyped thinking and hurtful bigotry have substantially declined, you may be forced to recognize that tolerance for differences continues to be an elusive dream. Indeed, hate can remain dormant in a culture, emerging without warning from the darkness in response to some threatening but enlightening episode or situation. In the week following the 1995 Oklahoma City bombing in which 168 people lost their lives, many Americans assumed that Middle-Eastern terrorists had been responsible. Before the real killer, Timothy McVeigh, could be arrested, news commentators and politicians had already implicated Middle-Eastern militants in the deadly attack. In response, there was an outbreak of anti-Muslim incidents—some 216 episodes of harassment, discrimination, and violence. But even when it was clear later on that the Oklahoma City attack was carried out by a White Christian lacking any ties to Muslim extremists, bigotry continued to make life miserable for Muslim Americans. In the workplace, some were fired for refusing to remove their head scarves ("hijabs") or taking breaks to pray. In schools, Muslim girls reported having their scarves yanked from their heads and being taunted by their classmates. In their neighborhoods, Muslims claimed to have been denied service at gas stations and grocery stores (Goodstein, 1996).

Similarly, during the tense months following the September 11 attack on America in 2001, Muslims and Arabs were the targets of violence perpetrated by angry Americans who looked in vain for the terrorists responsible for orchestrating 3000 deaths at the World Trade Center in New York City and at the Pentagon in Washington, D.C.

Not suprisingly, 9-11 brought with it an unprecedented number of hate offenses against Muslims. Specifically, in 2001, there was a 1600 percent increase in anti-Muslim hate crimes reported to local police departments. In 2000, Americans committed 28 hate offenses against their Muslim neighbors; in 2001, the number of such hate incidents rose to 481. Most (296 incidents) were acts of intimidation, but there were also 185 aggravated and simple assaults (Schevitz, 2002).

At least during the first weeks following 9-11, none of the hate-motivated offenses resulted in the murder of Muslim-Americans, though many Muslims were vandalized, intimidated, or assaulted. Ironically, however, Sikh Indians—who are neither Islamic nor Middle Eastern—became mistakenly targeted for death. Days after the attack on America, 49-year-old Balbir Singh Sodhi from Punjab, India was fatally shot as he did landscaping outside of his Mesa, Arizona, gas station. Sodhi's turban and long beard apparently reminded the killer of Osama bin Laden. As stated by a friend of the victim, Sikh Indians "are different people from Muslim people. We have different beliefs, a different religion" (CNN, 2001).

For the same reason that the number of anti-Muslim hate crimes soared, stereotyped attitudes toward Muslims also turned especially nasty following September 11, 2001. Opinion polls conducted by the *Washington Post* and ABC News indicated that some 33 percent of Americans regarded Islam in a negative light. Fourteen percent reported believing that Islam helps to inspire violence (Deane and Fears, 2006).

But more than five years later, in March 2006, the same pollsters found only a hardening in the attitudes of Americans toward Muslims. The unpopularity of the war in Iraq as well as major acts of terrorism against civilians in Spain and England linked to Islamic extremists apparently contributed to a growing distrust of Muslims in general. Forty-six percent of adult Americans told the pollsters that they now viewed Islam negatively; some 33 percent said that Islam helps to inspire violent behavior (Deane and Fears, 2006).

The September 11 attack on the United States also inspired a growing disdain for immigrants, especially those coming from Latin America. Xenophobia is nothing new. Even in the late nineteenth and early twentieth centuries, when most newcomers were European, some part of anti-immigrant sentiment reflected widespread fear of job loss. Whenever the jobless rate soared, so did the forces of nativism. But since September 11, 2001, as Americans have become increasingly anxious about the threat of international terrorism, stereotyped images of immigrants have turned decidely more negative. Myths and misconceptions about newcomers have assumed the status of cultural truisms. Anxious advocates of nativism envision huddled masses of impoverished, uneducated, disease-ridden criminals who sneak across our porous borders to steal jobs and murder our citizens (Levin and Rabrenovic, 2006).

In response, white supremacists and racist skinheads have committed a growing number of hate crimes against Latinos, both illegals and legals, both foreigners and American citizens. Masquerading as immigation reform groups, these fringe elements of the anti-immigrant movement have contributed to a climate of hate and violence (Anti-Defamation League, 2006). Moreover, when asked whether "you, a family member, or a close friend ever experienced discrimination because of your Latino or racial background," 47 percent of a national sample of Latinos responded in the affirmative (Time/Schulman, Ronca, and Bucuvalas, 2005).

Situations have also affected the level of anti-Semitism in the United States and in nations around the globe. Beginning especially in the year 2000, as the conflict in the Middle East between Israelis and Palestinians became increasingly more violent and intractable, the character of anti-Semitism in countries around the world was observed to change in ever more destructive and harmful ways. In what has come to be labeled the *new anti-Semitism,* Jews everywhere—even those who supported the establishment of a Palestinian state and had never even visited the Middle East—were now being held responsible for Israeli military policies (Chesler, 2003; Iganski and Kosman, 2003).

The second intifada or uprising of Palestinians began at the end of September 2000, in response to Israeli opposition leader Ariel Sharon's visit to a disputed area of Jerusalem in which both the Temple Mount and the Al-Aqsa Mosque are located. By October 7, as conflict between Israelis and Palestinians began to reach a fever pitch, Jews around the world became targets of anger and violence. In the United States alone, the number of anti-Semitic acts reached a peak, with some 259 incidents occurring during a 30-day period (Radler, 2001).

Unlike traditional forms of anti-Jewish bigotry associated with the White power movement and Nazi ideology, the new anti-Semitism was espoused not only by right-wing extremists but by proponents of progressive politics who voiced their opposition to all varieties of colonialism and racism. Many right-wingers in France and Germany regarded Jews, along with immigrants from Africa and the Middle East, as one element of the "foreign" influence in their countries responsible for the demise of European culture and an increase in the national unemployment rate. Many

American and British left-wingers saw Palestinians as victims and Israel as an oppressor state. When Middle-Eastern tensions rose—during the second Palestinian intifada in September 2000 and again in the spring of 2002 after the Israeli military occupied West Bank towns—the number of anti-Semitic attacks also increased (Chesler, 2003; Iganski and Kosmin, 2003). By 2003, there were more anti-Jewish hate attacks in European countries than at any time since World War II (Rosenblum, 2003). According to the Israeli government, more than 2500 French Jews had decided in 2002 to immigrate to Israel—the largest number since the 1967 war, and double the number who left France in 2001 (Frankel, 2003). In the United States, the level of anti-Semitism never escalated to the same degree as in European cities. Still, the Anti-Defamation League (2005) determined anti-Jewish incidents as being at their highest level in nine years. The League reported a total of 1821 incidents in 2004, representing a 17 percent rise over the 1557 incidents reported for 2003.

While the new anti-Semitism was spreading through both Europe and North America as well as the Islamic world, old fashioned forms of anti-Semitism also managed to find a niche in the thinking of Americans. In the immediate aftermath of presidential candidate Al Gore's selection of Senator Joseph Lieberman as his running mate in the 2000 election campaign, anti-Semitic messages appeared in chat rooms and online message boards around the Internet. On racist Web sites there were messages about ZOG (zionist occupied government), slurs about Lieberman's religion, and warnings about having a Jew in the White House (FNC, 2000).

Matthew Hale, the 27-year-old leader of World Church of the Creator, in a press release e-mailed to his proteges, said the following about the selection of Lieberman: "While undoubtedly some will be surprised by this, I am very happy that the Jew Joseph Lieberman has been chosen by Al Gore to be his running mate, for it brings the pervasive Jewish influence of the federal government out in the open so that people can see what we anti-Semites are talking about" (Anti-Defamation League, 2000).

Tom Metzger, who heads the White Aryan Resistance from his home in Falbrook, California, sent the following message to a mailing list of American Nazi Party members:

> The lusting for power and total control by the jew knows no limits and I can only pray that when the Jewish masters find a way to remove gore (if elected) and install the first jew president of the most powerful and bloodthirsty corporate empire in world history, that Lieberman and his controllers will institute every oppression that their twisted imaginations can invent, and aim them directly and solely at White MEN! (as quoted by Anti-Defamation League, 2000).

White extremists were not the only ones who reacted with anti-Semitism to the choice of a Jewish vice-presidential candidate. Lee

Alcorn, president of the National Association for the Advancement of Colored People (NAACP) in Dallas, Texas, told a radio audience that Black voters "need to be suspicious of any kind of partnerships between the Jews at that kind of level because we know that their interest primarily has to do with, you know, money and these kinds of things" (National Journal Group, 2000). Nation of Islam leader Louis Farrakhan warned that Lieberman's Jewish identity gives him "dual loyalty" to both the United States and the state of Israel.

Such anti-Semitic remarks about Lieberman are not the first expressions of hate and prejudice articulated by well-known Americans about specific minority Americans. Over the past few decades, beginning especially during the 1980s, Americans have been forced by circumstances to deal with people who are different, whether they liked it or not. During this period, almost unprecedented numbers of newcomers arrived from Asia and Latin America. More people of color began to participate in workplaces, neighborhoods, schools, and college dormitories, where they had been almost totally absent just a few decades earlier. In everyday life, we created more points of contact between groups whose members are different with respect to race, sexual orientation, and religion, forcing more Americans to give some thought to the possibility of retaliation and reprimand when they verbalized hateful remarks. Some might call it being politically correct, but it is really a result of the presence of groups whose members previously hadn't been around to object.

A Continuing Racial Gap

The continuing influence of hate in the lives of Americans is illustrated by the wide, perhaps widening, gap between Black and White Americans with respect to their worldviews. On both sides of the racial ledger, there are Americans who tend to be pessimistic about our future as a multicultural nation. Some even predict civil war. Before blowing up the federal building in Oklahoma City, Timothy McVeigh had secured the "blueprint" for his mass murder from a bigoted novel, *The Turner Diaries* (Macdonald, 1978), in which Americans battle the forces of evil represented by Jews, Blacks, and a communist-inspired federal government. White supremacists characterize Jews as "children of Satan" and Blacks and Latinos as "mud people" who exist at the spiritual and intellectual level of animals (Levin and McDevitt, 2002).

The cultural gap between Whites and Blacks can be seen in survey data that examine racial differences in Americans' explanations for inequality. Respondents from both racial groups tend to reject the idea that Blacks have less innate ability than Whites; both Whites and Blacks stress the need to equalize educational opportunities. But when asked to account for continuing Black disadvantage, the majority of Whites blame lack of motivation. In other words, Blacks don't make enough of an effort on their own behalf "to crawl out of the gutters of America." In sharp contrast, the majority of Blacks explain their own economic disadvantage as a result of persistent White discrimination or racism (Schuman et al., 1997), something that many White Americans deny. Indeed, regarding whether opportunities for Blacks exist in their local communities, the gap between Black and White opinions is large and persistent. For example, only 10 percent of all Whites report that Blacks are treated less fairly than Whites on the job; yet, 47 percent of all Blacks feel that way. Only 15 percent of all Whites say that Blacks are treated less fairly in stores downtown or in shopping malls; yet, 46 percent of all Blacks feel that way. Only 11 percent of Whites report that Blacks are treated less fairly in restaurants, bars, and theaters; yet, 39 percent of all Blacks feel that way. Only 30 percent of all Whites say that Blacks are treated less fairly by the police; yet, 64 percent of Blacks feel that way (Ludwig, 2000).

According to Patricia Turner (1993), the collective thinking of many Black Americans assumes the status of urban legends in which White Americans are seen as conspiring against them. Whereas most White Americans saw O. J. Simpson as his wife's murderer, the majority of Black Americans believed Simpson was not a perpetrator but an innocent victim of racist police officers who conspired to plant incriminating evidence against him. Similarly, many Blacks believe that nationwide restaurant chains add a secret ingredient to sterilize Black men, that soft drink companies are owned by the Ku Klux Klan, that the U.S. government's so-called war against drugs was actually waged as an excuse to incarcerate large numbers of young Black men, and that the U.S. military conspired to infect Africans with AIDS.

Unfortunately, the actions of our institutions too often give reason for Americans to be cynical and provide the evidence they need to maintain their conspiratorial beliefs. The fiascos at Ruby Ridge and Waco suggested to members of marginal groups that the FBI was just as evil as they had suspected. The disproportionately heavy sentences for possessing and dealing crack cocaine predictably assured that the war against drugs would bring under the control of the criminal justice system incredibly large numbers of Black men (Tonry, 1995). The widely held belief that law enforcement continues to discriminate against Black men was confirmed by several incidents of police brutality, profiling, and corruption in police departments around the country. In Philadelphia, for example, 300 cases were overturned or dismissed because police officers were thought to have planted evidence on Black suspects and lied at the trials of Black defendants (Janofsky, 1997). Moreover, Washington, D.C. law enforcement officials were caught sending hundreds of e-mail messages on their squad car computers that contained vulgar racist and homophobic references (Santana and Lengel, 2001).

Some of the racial skepticism of Black Americans has been translated into hate directed toward Whites, especially toward Catholics and Jews. A recent rally of thousands of Black youngsters in New York City was organized by Nation of Islam members who repeatedly referred to Jews as "bloodsuckers" and to the Pope as "a cracker."

The hostility of Americans of color toward Whites is by no means restricted to a relatively few radicals or professional discontents. A recent Harris survey of 3000 Americans sponsored by the National Conference for Community and Justice (2000) found that people of color and especially Black Americans have adopted a largely unflattering view of White Americans. More than 75 percent of all Black Americans reported believing that Whites are bigoted and prejudiced, bossy, and unwilling to share their inordinate wealth and power. More than 50 percent of all Latino Americans also share this view of White Americans.

The same Harris survey determined that Americans of color generally perceive that they lack opportunities open to Whites. Black Americans were especially dispirited, with 80 percent telling pollsters that they lack the same opportunities afforded to Whites. They felt especially unlikely to receive equal justice from the criminal justice system, including the police, to be promoted to a managerial position; to get loans and mortgages; and to be portrayed fairly by the media. To make matters worse, most White Americans reportedly disagree with the idea that people of color lack equal opportunities. In fact, a majority of Whites—in some cases climbing to almost 70 percent—said that Black Americans have equal access to a quality education, skilled jobs, decent housing, and loans and mortgages. Only in two relevant areas where Blacks perceive they are being denied equal treatment (in the media and by police) does a majority (and just barely so) of White Americans concur.

IS THE SIGNIFICANCE OF HATE ON THE DECLINE?

Social scientists have long sought to increase their understanding of the nature of hate—its origins, maintenance, and consequences. Many have expressed their concern about the debilitating impact of prejudice on the life-chances of minority-group members; on such attendant factors as confused self-identity, poor self-esteem, and serious sex-role conflicts (Pettigrew, 1964); and on what Smith (1995) has labeled "internal inferiorization." Others have focused their attention on what influence prejudice has on the quality of moral life for all Americans, majority and minority alike. In his classic work, *An American Dilemma*, Myrdal (1944) depicts American race relations as posing a major moral struggle for White America that is the result of a deeply rooted cultural conflict between the democratic values of the "American creed" and the social, political, and economic inequities experienced by Black Americans.

Social scientists have traditionally regarded prejudice and hate as destructive to society and to the individual. Directly or indirectly, prejudice causes innocent people to suffer, commits society's resources to antidemocratic if not unproductive ends, and does irreparable harm to the personality of the prejudiced individual. In the American experience alone, prejudice has been linked to a civil war, urban decay, crime and delinquency, and international tension.

The Environmental View

Another conception of prejudice, the *benign prejudice* viewpoint, has been advanced throughout history to explain the problems experienced by minority members of society. Instead of seeing hate and bigotry as causing poverty, unemployment, lack of education, and related social problems, the benign prejudice viewpoint locates the responsibility for inequality in characteristics of the minority group itself. From this standpoint, hate and prejudice are regarded as relatively harmless, secondary, or entirely irrelevant.

Some historians have suggested, for example, that throughout history, Jews have been at least partially responsible for their own ills. In his early writings, Lazare (1894, 1995) argued that throughout history (in ancient Alexandria, Rome, Persia, Turkey, the countries of Europe, or wherever else they settled), Jews remained apart, refusing to give up their beliefs and rituals or to assimilate into the mainstream of society. Instead, in whatever land to which they were deported, they sought to remain Jews by insisting on being able to practice their religion, to receive exemption from the customs of the majority, to remain separated from other inhabitants, and to govern themselves by their own laws. In ancient Rome and Alexandria, Jews were not required to appear in court or to market grain on a Saturday. In ancient Alexandria, they were permitted total self-governance, constituting a state within a state. In some countries, they were even exempted from paying taxes.

Such privileges, as well as the bond they shared as a separate religious community, combined to give Jewish residents special opportunities for engaging in trade and accumulating wealth. But such opportunities also engendered widespread jealousy and envy that in turn created large-scale animosity toward them among the local inhabitants. Ancient Greeks and Romans were already covetous of the advantages that permitted Jews to carry on trade under favorable economic circumstances. The wealth of the Jew, it was said, was gained by deception, fraud, and oppression at the expense of the Christian (Lazare, 1894, 1995).

Over the course of his career, Lazare's benign prejudice view of anti-Semitism was gradually modified to take into account the historical impact of victimization on the Jewish experience. For one thing, he came to understand that much of the separateness of Jewish life was not self-imposed but originated in discrimination from the wider society. However they behaved in relation to the dominant inhabitants, Jews were treated as slaves and pariahs. During the Crusades, the presence of Jewish citizens who refused to convert to Catholicism was regarded as a symbolic threat by religious zealots who sought to spread their theology across the continent. Jews who refused to convert were massacred.

During the Middle Ages, Jews were systematically excluded from many respectable ways of making a living such as owning land, farming, or being craftspeople. Because of its importance to society, however, the dreaded role of usurer, a role despised on religious grounds by the Catholic majority, was granted to Jews by default. In Spain, Jews were forced at the threat of death or exile to practice their religion secretly, masquerading in public places as converted Christians. In seventeenth- and eighteenth-century Germany, Jews were at best second-class citizens who lacked many of the rights afforded other inhabitants. In Polish cities, Jews were prohibited from living among the Christian population and were forced to live in ghettos. By the middle of the twentieth century, long after the death of historian Bernard Lazare, German anti-Semitism had turned decidedly racist, so much so that even total conversion to Christianity would not have protected a Jew from paying the ultimate price.

Despite compelling evidence to indicate the malignancy of racism, some social scientists have implied, if not explicitly stated, that prejudice can no longer be held accountable for the poverty, miseducation, or underemployment presently experienced by members of certain groups in our society. Their argument usually runs as follows: Although initially responsible for the problems of a group (e.g., back in the days of slavery), prejudice or racism of the majority is no longer to blame. Current prejudice is regarded as benign. The minority group is viewed as trapped in a self-feeding vicious circle of deprivation that is difficult if not impossible to reverse. Ryan (1971) regarded this view in the most negative sense possible as blaming the victim; others see it as a refreshing change from a viewpoint that has led us nowhere fast in our efforts to reduce various inequalities.

According to Ryan, the most common form of blaming the victim involves the cultural deprivations to which a minority-group member is presumably exposed. As a case in point, Ryan considers an inner-city child who is blamed for his own miseducation. The focus here is on the alleged defects of the child: his lack of exposure to books and magazines, the absence of encouragement or support from his parents, and his own impulsiveness. By confining attention to the child and to deficiencies in his home environment, it is possible to overlook the

> . . . collapsing buildings and torn textbooks, the frightened, insensitive teachers, the six additional desks in the room, the blustering, frightened principals, the relentless segregation, the callous administrator, the irrelevant curriculum, the bigoted or cowardly members of the school board, the insulting history books, the stingy taxpayers, the fairy-tale readers, or the self-serving faculty of the local teachers' college. (Ryan, 1971, p. 4)

To explain the persistence of socioeconomic inequalities between groups, some social scientists have posited the existence of a culture of poverty (Lewis, 1968), a way of life that includes shared views about desirable and undesirable behavior as well as adaptational techniques and institutions for coping with the problems of a lower-class existence. But such a conception of a culture of poverty depicts more than just a way of adapting to a set of conditions imposed by the dominant group. Once it becomes widely accepted, the culture of poverty, because of its influence on children, tends to maintain itself from one generation to the next. By the age of 6 or 7, children have usually internalized the values and norms of their subculture, making them incapable of taking full advantage of the opportunities that may become available to them during their lifetime (Lewis, 1968, p. 188).

Since Lewis's analysis in the 1960s, the notion of a vicious circle of cultural deprivation to account for inequalities between dominant and minority groups has gained rather wide acceptance among social scientists and laypersons alike. The late Daniel Patrick Moynihan gave it official recognition when as U.S. assistant secretary of labor (long before he became a senator from New York) he asserted in his so-called Moynihan Report that it was not hate or racism but the deterioration of the Black family that was the fundamental source of the economic weaknesses in the Black community (1965).

More recently, the benign prejudice view has been articulated forcefully by both Blacks and Whites in an attempt to explain the perpetuation of racial inequality into the twenty-first century. During the summer of 2004, comedian Bill Cosby, who himself is Black, told an audience of Black activists in Chicago that Black teenagers are the "dirty laundry" in the Black community because of their "poor grammar, foul language, and rude manners" (Harris and Farhi, 2004, A1). Rather than focus on racist practices and policies in the wider society, Cosby pointed the finger squarely at the high rates of teen pregnancy and illiteracy characterizing impoverished Black teenagers.

Larry Elder (2000), an attorney who hosts a courtroom series on national television and writes a syndicated newspaper column, similarly blamed the continuation of disproportionate poverty in the Black community on the fact that 70 percent of all Black children are born out of wedlock, a figure that is almost three times larger than the level decried in the Moynihan Report. Elder suggested that scholarships and other forms of financial aid to impoverished students will be wasted if the recipients lack the "discipline" and "character" to work hard when they don't want to. And these, he said, are values that are instilled in the home, especially in a home in which both mother and father are present and capable of raising their children in an effective manner.

John McWhorter (2000, 2005), professor of linguistics at the University of California, Berkeley, similarly claims to locate the source of Black academic underachievement in certain themes running through Black subculture rather than in White racism. The first theme he calls the *cult of victimology*, whereby Black Americans focus on their victimhood as an identity to be nurtured and preserved instead of a problem to be solved. The second he refers to as *separatism*, which encourages Black Americans to see themselves as a distinct and separate group whose members are morally exempt from the rules of behavior governing the lives of others. The third theme McWhorter identifies as *anti-intellectualism*, whereby Black youngsters associate academic success and learning for learning's sake as being characteristic of White America and therefore as not appropriate to their lives. According to McWhorter, these three cultural themes represent a form of collective "self-sabotage." Together, they assure that Black Americans will continue to perform badly both in and out of the classroom, even in the absence of large-scale racial discrimination.

Criminologist James Q. Wilson (1992) takes a benign prejudice viewpoint by blaming racism on the high crime rate among Black Americans and Latinos. In light of the elevated rate of crime committed by Black Americans, he argues, it only makes sense that White Americans would be fearful of Black Americans. According to Wilson, White racism will come down to the extent that Black crime also comes down.

Taking a contrary point of view, Russell (1998) takes Wilson to task for the narrowness of his view of the relationship between Black crime and White racism. Russell suggests that Whites' fear of Blacks and Latinos has a basis in more than just a high crime rate. Whites also are fearful that Blacks will take their jobs, contaminate White popular culture (its music, dress, and language), overpopulate the country, and exact a measure of revenge for their treatment by White America. Russell also argues that Wilson's view of the relationship between Black crime and White racism is simplistic and ahistorical, ignoring the interrelationships of crime, poverty, and education, as well as the impact of slavery. In other words, Wilson's view has reversed the order of cause and effect: crime doesn't cause racism; racism causes a high crime rate. This viewpoint—that a disproportionate level of Black crime is a result of economic and social disadvantage and discrimination—is shared by most criminologists, although not those who take a benign prejudice position.

Some versions of benign prejudice form the basis of a policy of "benign neglect." If the responsibility for Black and Latino poverty can be located in the one-parent Black family or the Black subculture, then why bother enacting policies and programs designed to eradicate poverty? If the blame for White racism can be located in a high crime rate among Blacks, then why enact policies to reduce discrimination and prejudice?

At the same time, the benign prejudice perspective can instead be employed to justify policies of affirmative action and preferential treatment designed to level the playing field for minorities who have suffered from past discrimination. Such policies do not necessarily aim to reduce current racism; they try to make up for previous inequities. For example, court-ordered busing during the 1970s in Boston schools was meant to make up for a history of decisions made by the Boston school committee purposely meant to keep the city's schools segregated by race. Similarly recognizing the inequalities in the educational experiences of Blacks and Whites (not to mention the educational value of a diverse student body), affirmative action policies in colleges and universities sought to encourage growth in the enrollment of students of color.

It should also be noted that efforts to improve school dropout rates and rates of teen pregnancy do not necessarily preclude efforts to reduce discriminatory policies in the wider society. The most effective response to group inequities, it might be argued, would be to do both.

The Hereditary View

Another version of benign prejudice has developed from the work of those who assume a genetic basis of group differences in intelligence. The idea that heredity plays a major role in determining human intelligence has been around for more than a century. In 1883, Galton, who made a study of family eminence, suggested that "the instincts and faculties of different men differ almost as profoundly as animals in different cages of the zoological gardens."

During the early part of the twentieth century, psychologists found that immigrants coming from Poland, Russia, Greece, Turkey, and Italy tended to score lower on intelligence tests than immigrants coming from northwestern Europe. Because of group differences, these psychologists argued that "Mediterranean-Latin-Slavic people" must be genetically stupid and that admitting them to the United States in large numbers would pollute the stream of national intelligence. This finding became a basis for the restrictive immigration laws of the 1920s (Kamin, 1973).

The argument that minority group members are genetically inferior is by no means a new one, but over the past few decades there has been renewed interest in it in the United States. For many, the re-emergence of this view in social science is associated with Arthur Jenson, an educational psychologist who revised the hypothesis that "genetic factors are strongly implicated in the average Negro-White intelligence difference"

(1969, p. 82). In a subsequent article, Richard Herrnstein (1971) similarly suggested that socioeconomic status may be based on inherited differences in intelligence, permitting the development of an *hereditary meritocracy for American society* in which intellectually superior individuals will rule.

In a particularly distressing version of the benign prejudice viewpoint, J. Philippe Rushton (2001), an evolutionary psychologist from the University of Western Ontario, has suggested that racial differences in such advantageous traits as family stability, ability to postpone gratification, sexual restraint, and law-abiding behavior are actually a result of differences in brain size and weight. Asians are at the top of the positive trait scale and also have larger and heavier brains, Caucasians are in the middle on advantageous traits and brain size, and Africans are at the bottom on both counts.

Rushton's viewpoint has never had great impact on popular culture, although abridged versions of his books have been circulated to a wide range of social scientists. A best-selling book entitled *The Bell Curve* by Richard Herrnstein and Charles Murray (1994) focused the attention of the nation once again on racial differences in intelligence. In particular, these behavioral scientists reported, among other things, that the average Black American has a lower IQ than the average White or Asian American, and that this IQ gap is largely inherited.

The title of Murray and Herrnstein's book, *The Bell Curve,* evokes an image of scientific impartiality and precise neutrality. Yet, given the present stage of our knowledge about human behavior, it remains all but impossible to draw unbiased conclusions about racial differences in intelligence. One thing seems certain: Americans need guidance in how to wipe out the really important problems that divide us as a people—lack of opportunity, educational inequality, hopelessness, and bigotry. Only when these vital differences have been held constant will racial differences in intelligence be made clear. In some future society in which equality of opportunity is truly a reality, we may not need social scientists to justify selfishness. In the meantime, we might turn our attention to do what is possible to make our social environment conducive to maximizing the potential of all citizens, regardless of race, religion, sexual orientation, gender, disability status, or ethnic origin.

Common-sense observations highlight the absurdity of claims as to the immutability of IQ. In 1923, psychologist Carl Brigham, using the results of IQ testing, concluded that 83 percent of Jews, 80 percent of Hungarians, and 70 percent of Italians were feeble-minded and should consequently be excluded from citizenship in the United States. Notwithstanding the current widespread belief that Jews are an intelligent (perhaps too intelligent, according to the stereotype) people overall, Brigham argued then that Jews have the color, stature, mental abilities, and head form of their Alpine neighbors, what he referred to as a "race of peasants" who make perfect slaves and serfs.

Ironically, the Jewish experience in America provides us with one of the most compelling arguments for the environmental instead of the hereditary basis for intelligence. During the 1920s, when Brigham singled out Jews for scoring relatively low on IQ tests, Jews were also concentrated in the lower classes along with other impoverished newcomers to America. By contrast, today's Jewish Americans tend to score among the very highest groups on various tests of intelligence, not coincidentally at the same time that their wealth, power, and status have also seen major improvement. This leaves the unmistakable impression that changes in socioeconomic status are responsible for changes in the way that Jews and, of course, other groups score on IQ tests (Smith, 1995).

Any scientific conclusion, or even hypothesis, concerning genetically determined racial differences in ability or potential is also a political statement with potentially serious political consequences. Scientists who proclaim the inequality of the races have been cited by attorneys in desegregation cases and by legislators with respect to appropriations bills. During economic hard times, such ideas seem to gain in credibility. Members of the dominant group seek to justify cutting back government spending programs to minority Americans in the areas of education and welfare. If the overrepresentation of inner-city Blacks in poverty can be traced to some problem in their environment or heredity (rather than to centuries of discrimination), there is no reason to throw additional government resources at such programs. As Smith (1995) correctly notes, many policy makers and academics enjoy good reputations although they have adopted this benign prejudice viewpoint. But one must wonder what impact the bell curve crowd has had on the self-concept of Black Americans who repeatedly hear from the so-called scientific community that in relation to Whites and Asians they are stupid, incompetent, and lacking intellectually. Even more insidious, the bell curve debate has had its analogue in the racial images outside the academy where people of color struggle on a daily basis with the unflattering messages they receive from members of the dominant group. Thus, some White cab drivers won't stop for a Black man and some White women won't share an elevator ride with one. When some Black men drive through a White neighborhood, they are prepared to be stopped by a suspicious police officer who uses some sort of racial profile that treats all Blacks as drug dealers and smugglers; when they go shopping downtown, Blacks are followed through stores by security guards who see them as potential shoplifters. According to a recent study, Blacks and Latinos are twice as likely as Whites to report that the police used or threatened force against them. Moreover, Black drivers are more likely to be pulled over and Black and Latino drivers are more likely to be searched, handcuffed, or ticketed (Gullo, 2001). More than four of every ten Black Americans report having been the victims of racial profiling, including almost three-quarters of young Black males (Newport, 1999).

This is one of the reasons why so many Black Americans cringed in horror when in 1995, they saw O. J. Simpson's courtroom appearances in his murder trial being telecast daily to a national audience. It isn't only that Blacks mistrust the criminal justice system (in cities like Philadelphia and Los Angeles, police officers have been charged with planting evidence on Black suspects), Blacks were also concerned that the publicity surrounding the Simpson murder trial would reinforce the afrophobic stereotype by which they were being personally judged, on an everyday basis, to be thugs and rapists. Even if the environmental version of benign prejudice has a degree of validity, and it probably does, there is reason to believe that hate and prejudice continue to feed the vicious circle in which many Black Americans have been trapped.

Stereotyping has more than a material effect on its victims. Especially in situations in which little or nothing is known, on a first-hand basis, about an individual—in shops and stores, elevators, real estate offices, cabs, college campuses, factories, restaurants, large companies, and the criminal justice system—minority members may be treated stereotypically as a matter of routine (Lee, Jussim, and McCauley, 1995). Moreover, the fear of confirming negative stereotypes about their own group can seriously erode the ability of minority group members to achieve their potential. In one series of studies, Black students who were given a difficult test of their verbal abilities performed well except when they were asked to report their race and they were made to believe that doing poorly would confirm the stereotypic belief that Blacks are intellectually inferior to Whites (Steele and Aronson, 1995). Not only can the threat of being stereotyped reduce an individual's performance, but it can also cause an individual to avoid those areas of life in which she is expected to fail (Crocker and Major, 1989; Steele, 1992). Concerned about confirming the stereotype that they are less intelligent than Whites, some Black children over time tend to disconnect academic achievement with self-image. They come to associate learning for learning's sake and academic achievement as within the province of White America and not within their own. In the long run, the acceptance of this anti-intellectual attitude profoundly reduces Black children's ability to compete in any arena where the ability to learn is essential (Osborne, 1995).

It should be noted that some psychologists have shown certain stereotypes to have a degree of accuracy (Lee, Jussim, and McCauly, 1995). For example, it is indeed true that 53 percent of all homicides are committed by Black Americans, who represent only 12 percent of the population of the United States. Knowing of the overrepresentation of Blacks in violent crime does not, however, answer the important question as to *why* Black Americans are overrepresented among violent criminals. To explain this phenomenon, one might examine the impact of poverty, discrimination, social disorganization, racism, strain, and other factors that have been demonstrated to serve as direct causes of criminal behavior found disproportionately among Black Americans. For those who are eager to apply a genetic explanation to Black violent crime, it should be emphasized that the rate of serious violence committed by Black Americans has not remained constant. It has risen and fallen dramatically over many decades. The same is true of other groups in society whose crime rates have varied significantly over the years. In the nineteenth century, impoverished Irish immigrants were overrepresented among street criminals; during the 1920s, it was impoverished Italian and Jewish Americans who became identified with gangland killings.

Some White Americans, concerned about their personal safety, might argue that knowing that 53 percent of all murders are perpetrated by Blacks is important information with which to avoid their own victimization. From this viewpoint, the argument might be that they should avoid Blacks to reduce their chances of being killed. The problem with this kind of thinking is that it ignores a couple of important points. First, that murder tends to be intraracial—Black perpetrators kill Blacks; Asian perpetrators kill Asians; Latino perpetrators kill Latinos; and White perpetrators kill Whites.

Second, and even more important, although it is true that more than half of all murders are committed by Blacks, this does not mean that more than half of all Blacks commit murder. In fact, only 25 in every 100,000 Black Americans have killed anyone, leaving 99,975 in every 100,000 who have not. Just to put the predictability issue in comparative perspective, we might use the same logic to suggest that any individual would be far safer if he were totally to avoid all men. After all, not 53 percent but a truly shocking 90 percent of all murders are committed by men rather than women. Once again, however, the logic of this approach to predictability leads us astray. Only 12 in every 100,000 men ever kill anyone. Like the overwhelming majority of Blacks, most men are law-abiding citizens, not murderers.

Acting on the anti-Black stereotype is therefore not at all an effective predictor and is tantamount to treating most Blacks as murderers for the sins of a few. Most people do not like to be stereotyped; instead, they seek to be treated as unique individuals with their own sets of strengths and weaknesses and of accomplishments and failures. It would make vastly more sense for the purposes of reducing the likelihood of being harmed to avoid any man or woman who has a history of being dangerous and violent, whether they are Black, White, Latino, or Asian.

Not that particular characteristics of groups don't have some bearing on the way they are treated by members of the dominant group. It's just that these characteristics may themselves still be a result of their treatment. The vicious circle of deprivation is no closed system. It often begins with discrimination and exploitation and ends with more of the same

(Patterson, 1998). During the Middle Ages, Jews were systematically excluded from respectable occupations and restricted to the role of money-lending. Their consequent overrepresentation in fields of finance and banking was later used to confirm the stereotype that Jews are money-grubbing and mercenary as well as to justify efforts to grant them only second-class citizenship or to expel them from the countries in which they had lived since birth. Similarly, when their land was deemed important for White Americans to possess, American Indians were forcibly expelled from their homes to be transplanted to impoverished reservations where their opportunities for economic progress became almost nonexistent. Any armed resistance on their part was then used to prove that Indians were barbaric savages who deserved whatever fate they were given. And Black Americans were initially enslaved and subsequently became the recipients of Jim Crow laws that until the 1960s kept them separated from Whites in most areas of public life. The Black subculture that arose out of their legal and *de facto* segregation over many generations has been thought by some White Americans to be the primary source of Black economic disadvantage. It is easy enough to put blinders on and ignore the historical role of hate and prejudice in determining the life chances of an entire people.

CONCLUSION

Notwithstanding the decline in its public expression since World War II, hate continues to dictate the terms of intergroup conflict in the United States. In certain circles, prejudice has become more subtle and sophisticated. Among some, it may exist only on an unconscious level. In others, it remains dormant until such time that the advantaged status of the dominant group is challenged. At this point, the stereotyped image of the "outsiders" is brought forth to justify doing them harm.

There is a large and apparently growing number of social scientists who believe that hate or prejudice is no longer responsible for racial inequalities. Instead, they blame some characteristic of the victims' culture or heredity. Although the benign prejudice viewpoint alerts us to the possibility of environmental sources of inequality, there is every reason to believe that hate continues to play an important role in causing cultural changes that contribute to racial disadvantage. As espoused by the bell curve advocates, the hereditary view of racial inferiority may have an impact of its own in sending a message to people of color, especially to Black Americans, suggesting that they cannot possibly improve their ability to achieve educational or economic parity no matter how hard they try. Unfortunately, this seems to be the same message that many Black Americans get every day from ordinary White Americans who sincerely believe that they are not prejudiced.

CHAPTER 2

■ ■ ■ ■ ■ ▬▬▬▬▬▬▬▬▬▬▬▬▬▬▬▬▬▬▬▬▬▬

A TYPOLOGY OF HATE

CRIMES OF HATE

Hate crimes are committed against individuals because these people are perceived to be different in some socially significant way. The FBI collects data on hate offenses based on differences in race, religion, ethnicity/ national origin, sexual orientation, and disability status.[1]

Prior to the 1990s, before the FBI began to gather hate crime data at a national level, our primary source of hate crime statistics consisted of reports issued by advocacy groups such as the Anti-Defamation League (ADL) and the Southern Poverty Law Center. Although valuable to researchers, such data were also regarded with suspicion by some legal scholars who argued that the ADL and other advocacy organizations had a vested interest in reporting growing numbers (Jacobs and Henry, 1996; Jacobs and Potter, 1997; Jacobs and Potter, 1998). The FBI's more recent effort to collect data on hate-motivated offenses has also had its detractors. Like other aspects of the Uniform Crime Reports, hate crime incidents, offenders, and victims are voluntarily reported by local jurisdictions to the FBI.

Even as late as 2004, there were still some police jurisdictions that simply refused to cooperate. At the same time, the percentage of jurisdictions voluntarily reporting hate offenses has gradually increased since the early 1990s. Most of the population of the United States is now covered in nationally reported hate crime statistics.

In 2004, the most recent year for which hate crime data are available at the national level, there were only five hate-motivated murders reported to the FBI (2005). On the other hand, some 62 percent of all of the thousands of hate crimes reported annually were directed not against property but against persons, most of which took the form of intimidations and assaults. The location of hate crime incidents varied, but they

---

[1]In some states, gender is also included among those characteristics protected by hate crime statutes, but it is not counted among hate offenses reported nationally.

seemed to be concentrated in homes, on the streets, and in schools and colleges. Race was the most common basis for committing a hate offense against a victim, with anti-Black attacks most likely to occur and anti-White attacks in second place. Anti-Jewish, anti-Muslim, and anti-gay followed by anti-Latino and anti-Asian offenses were also prevalent. A wide range of groups was represented among the victims of hate crimes. Among them were people with physical and mental disabilities, bisexuals, Protestants, Catholics, and American Indians.

This chapter focuses on the motivations and circumstances of the people who commit hate crimes as well as on the people who encourage and support them. The typology presented here not only encompasses but is also much broader than the hardened hatemongers and dabblers in hate who are directly responsible for attacking people who are different (Levin and McDevitt, 1993, 1995b). In addition, the typology includes those who sit on the sidelines, the sympathizers and spectators, without whom crimes of hate would be far less problematic.

HATEMONGERS

When a sadistic offense is committed because a victim is different, there seems to be much reason to suggest that the motivation contains important elements of hate. Sadism is essentially designed to give a perpetrator a sense of power, control, and dominance, but at the expense of a set of victims. The three White supremacists who were charged with James Byrd's murder in Jasper, Texas—John King, Lawrence Brewer, and Shawn Berry—beat the Black hitchhiker until he was unconscious, chained him to their pickup truck, and then dragged him down the road on his back for almost three miles to his death. For the first two miles, not only was Byrd alive, but he was also conscious. Only when he was decapitated by a boulder at the side of the road was the victim's suffering ended and his life mercifully taken.

The Role of Organized Hate

Investigators discovered a Ku Klux Klan manual among the possessions carried by one of the suspects; and two of the suspects wore White supremacist body tattoos depicting the Confederate Knights of America. King, Brewer, and Berry were definitely ardent admirers of the Klan who used White supremacist propaganda and enjoyed being identified with White supremacist symbols of power.

In addition to the murder of James Byrd, there have been several high-profile hate crimes over the past few years committed by the members of White supremacist organizations (Fox and Levin, 2006). In August 1999, Buford Furrow walked into a Jewish Community Center in the Los Angeles area and opened fire on a group of children as they played. Although he failed in his attempt to kill his young victims, Furrow then shot to death a Filipino letter carrier who just happened to be in the wrong place at the wrong time. A photograph later released to the public showed Furrow a few years earlier dressed in a Nazi uniform at the Hayden, Idaho, compound of the racist organization known as Aryan Nations.

As a cultural phenomenon, there are literally millions of Americans who, in varying degrees, dislike the members of various minority groups in society. Most of them would, however, never even think of committing an act of violence against someone because they are different. The relationship between hate and violence is far from perfect. Hate can and does occur without violence; violence against outsiders can and does occur in the absence of hate.

Organized hate groups provide the situational facilitators in whose presence hate violence becomes more likely to occur. Not unlike a gang or a cult, the organized hate group comes to represent the family of a newly recruited member. Typically, the members of organized hate groups have lacked a sense of belonging. They aren't getting along with their parents, can't make it at school with their peers, and are forced to take dead-end jobs, at best. Many of them are unemployed or work in dead-end jobs as manual laborers (Borgeson, 2006). But in Posse Comitatus, Aryan Nations, National Alliance Creativity Movement, or the Klan, they gain what has been missing in their lives, a sense of belonging and a vague feeling of their own importance. Hatemongers espouse hate and violence, but their underlying motivation is more complex (Ezekiel, 1995).

In social psychology, it is well known that the group can make the difference between attitude and action, between thinking about violence and actually perpetrating it. Acting in a group rather than alone reduces feelings of personal responsibility. Because blame or responsibility is shared, it is also weakened. Individuals may be willing to take more risks, to engage in dangerous behavior, simply because they don't feel that they can be held accountable for their actions.

Hate from a Distance

No more than 5 percent of all hate crimes nationally are committed by members of organizations like the Ku Klux Klan, Aryan Nations, or the White Aryan Resistance. Still, groups of White supremacists continue behind the scenes to inspire murder, assault, and vandalism. They encourage and support much larger numbers of violent offenses committed by nonmembers who may be totally unsophisticated with respect to the ideology of hate—racist skinheads, alienated teenagers, hate-filled young men looking to have a good time at someone else's expense (Levin and McDevitt, 1993).

While serving time behind bars for burglary convictions, two of the suspects in Jasper apparently had links with the Aryan Brotherhood, a prison hate group whose members are often recruited by White supremacists after they have been released. Established in many states around the country, the Aryan Brotherhood introduces inmates to the theology of the Identity Church, according to which a race war is inevitable. Prison may be a school for crime, but it is also a crash course in hatred and a training ground for leaders of the most dangerous White supremacist groups in our society.

Hatemongers often retaliate in an organized fashion. They want more than just to stop a particular event from happening or a particular individual from intruding; they believe that the very presence of certain groups of people in *their* town, *their* state, *their* country represents an intolerable threat to their personal well-being and to the survival of their group's way of life. Hatemongers provide propaganda to individuals looking to justify their own hateful behavior; they train youngsters in the art of bashing minorities; they recruit on college campuses and in prisons and workplaces; and they operate cable-access television programs featuring interviews with one another. These are the Americans who join Posse Comitatus, The Identity Church, The White Aryan Resistance, the Ku Klux Klan, the National Socialist Movement, and the like. There aren't many who qualify as hatemongers, but the few who do are responsible for some of the most vicious acts of violence perpetrated against citizens (Levin and McDevitt, 1993).

Biblical Bigotry

The underlying religious inspiration for many organized hate groups is provided by the Christian Identity Church, a worldwide movement whose ministers preach that those who call themselves Jews are actually the children of the devil and that Blacks, Latinos, and Asians are "mud people" whose spiritual development remains at the level of animals rather than human beings. According to the Identity Church, the true Israelites in the Bible are the ancestors of those Americans who came from northern European countries.

White Aryan hatemongers are not the only ones who preach biblical bigotry. The beliefs of the Black Hebrew Israelites bear a remarkable resemblance to the theology of Christian Identity practiced by many White supremacists. Members of the Black movement depict themselves as divinely blessed by God with moral superiority; they are God's authentic chosen people of the Old Testament. They see Whites as blue-eyed devils and conventional Jews as imposters.

Black Hebrew Israelites who have migrated from the United States to Israel are usually peaceful. In America, however, they are known by the police for their violence and criminal activities, due in large part to the Miami-based Nation of Yahweh that was headed by Yahweh Ben Yahweh. In the 1980s, members of the Nation of Yahweh, under the direction of the man they thought of as the Messiah, committed several homicides (Levin and Fox, 1991).

As do the Christian Identify group and certain civilian militia groups, Black Hebrew Israelites draw on the Khazarian legend to explain why those who refer to themselves as Jews are actually imposters. The Kingdom of Khazaria, one of the most diverse countries of medieval Europe, existed in an area of what is known now as southern Russia. In the eighth century, Bulan, who was the king of Khazaria, adopted Judaism. In one version of the story, he was forced to become Jewish after his kingdom was invaded by Jewish tribes from the Crimean Peninsula. In another version, Bulan voluntarily converted to Judaism only after carefully considering the relative merits of Islam, Christianity, and Judaism. Soon afterwards, Khazarian aristocrats also converted and Judaism became the official religion of the kingdom of Khazaria, although other religions were also tolerated. Most Khazarians became Jews, but some converted to Islam or Christianity. The appeal of Judaism may have been enhanced by the fact that Khazaria had, at the same time, become a destination for substantial numbers of persecuted Jews from Europe and Asia who sought a safe haven (Brook, 1999).

After 250 years, the medieval kingdom of Khazaria was overrun by Russian soldiers. Those Jews who remained in Khazaria were forcibly baptized. The remainder fled to Hungary, Ukraine, Lithuania, Belarus, Slovakia, Romania, Poland, and parts of Russia (Brook, 1999).

The existence of the kingdom of Khazaria is an indisputable historical fact. Yet most of the details surrounding the association of Eastern European Jews with Khazaria and the dissolution of the kingdom constitute unsubstantiated legend wholeheartedly adopted by organizations and individuals—members of the Black Hebrew Israelites, Christian Identity, and some militia groups—eager to discredit Judaism and to substantiate their conspiratorial views concerning the Jewish people. They argue that the origins of most of European or Ashkenazi Jewry can be traced back to the kingdom of Khazarian and not to Jerusalem. Thus, from this viewpoint, European Jews were converted and therefore cannot make claims to the land of Israel (Patriot Fax Network, 1996).

One part of the legend supports the notion that Jews seek to control the world's peoples. Their claim is that for more than 1000 years, ever since the dissolution of the Khazarian kingdom and the dispersion of

European Jews throughout the world, Khazarians have passed along to their offspring a secret plot to amass great wealth and political power and ultimately to take over all of the countries around the world (Patriot Fax Network, 1996).

For anti-Semites both Black and White, the term "Khazarian" serves more than one purpose. First, the Khazarian legend traces in detail the historical basis for the centuries old charge that Jews represent an international conspiracy to gain control over the world's economic resources. Second, the term "Khazarian" (as a replacement for "Jew") has become a codeword for those who do not wish to be accused of anti-Semitism. They are not anti-Jewish, only anti-Khazarian. Third, the term "Khazarian" has greater scope than Ashkenazi Jew, including within it not only all Jews of European descent but also certain Christians and Muslims who are considered the enemies of freedom and whose ancestry can be traced back to Eastern Europe (remember that some Khazarians converted to Christianity and Islam). Thus, some opponents of the concept of a "one-world order" identify the Rockefeller family and former president George Bush as non-Jewish Khazarians. Finally, focusing on Khazarians also lends credibility to the accusation that Jews, especially Ashkenazi Jews, represent a racial group rather than just a religion. Treating Jews as a race becomes important to those who argue that they are a breed apart from the rest of humanity and must be eliminated rather than converted to Christianity.

The Militia Movement and White Supremacy

A few years ago, I spent the day in a small town north of Boston at a "Patriot Potluck" attended by 75 members of the so-called Patriot movement—militia members, survivalists, and other political discontents who listened attentively to the words of a long list of speakers. The first and featured speaker was a leader of the militia movement in New Hampshire, Ed Brown, who spoke among other things about the evils of the Khazarians. As he warned the audience to be on guard, a voice in the audience could clearly be heard to agree with Brown's cautionary words. "Right, Ed," said the man in the crowd. "It's the Ashkenazi." Brown immediately admonished him about using the word "Ashkenazi." "Stick to the term Khazarian," he advised. "They are the true source of evil."

Militias have been linked, at least in the public mind, with everything from the Oklahoma City massacre in which 168 people lost their lives to Atlanta's Olympics pipebomb murder. According to the stereotyped version, militia members are nothing more than a collection of gun-loving hatemongers and thugs who preach first and second amendment rights as an excuse for waging war against the federal government. And I am certain that there are some militia members who fit the image. But that is also why I was so surprised when the 75 men, women, and children at the Patriot potluck I attended seemed so hospitable and friendly, even innocuous.

The first thing that struck me about this gathering was its diversity in terms of age, social class, and geography. They were men, women, and children from several states who hardly resembled the image I had expected to see. From a distance, in fact, they could easily have been mistaken for a group of bridge players or a convention of social workers.

I was also surprised by the utter boredom of their speeches. Through a five-hour procession, I heard almost nothing about guns and bombs and a great deal about financial hardship and economic disaster. Speaker after speaker after speaker talked about money and how to keep it or make more of it—about how to defeat the IRS through Common Law Courts, about how to withdraw from the Social Security system, about the effect of free trade on the unemployment rate, and about how to avoid going into debt. I got the strong impression that these were Americans who had suffered through hard times and were looking for some way to survive. Their response was to blame the federal government, the UN, the so-called one-world order, the communists, and international bankers. Some, but by no means all of them, also blamed Jews, Blacks, Asians, and Latinos (Levin, 1997a).

If there is a bit of overlap between militia groups and White supremacists, it is because both believe that the federal government has let them down. Both have committed themselves to the defense of their version of America. The militia movement gained dramatically in both membership and publicity during the deep recession of the early 1980s, at a time when much of the attention of the nation was on big city problems. Some militia members came from the ranks of automobile workers who lost their jobs in Detroit's massive layoffs, but many more had been miners, farmers, ranchers, and people in the timber business who had been put out of business, who simply could no longer make ends meet, and who were looking for help from government officials—help that never came or came too late to make a difference. In addition, some militia groups were convinced that communists had taken over all branches of the federal government and that the United Nations and one-world order types were conspiring to rob the United States of its sovereignty.

So concerned are militia members about the erosion of their constitutional rights that they stand ready and willing to defend our country against itself. They often cite what they regard as a federally instigated conflagration at Waco, Texas, and before that the killing by federal agents of the wife and son of a White supremacist at Ruby Ridge, Idaho, as proof that the government is out to get its citizens. They refuse to give up their firearms, believing that they might very well need all the weapons they can get to resist the coming onslaught by foreign and communist forces. Some hate Jews and Blacks, but there are also Jewish and Black militia members.

Not unlike militia groups, the members of organized hate groups like the Klan, Posse Comitatus, Aryan Nations, World Church of the Creator, and White Aryan Resistance also despise the federal government, but for different if overlapping reasons. They refer to the federal government as ZOG (Zionist Occupied Government) and they emphasize their belief that Jews and Blacks have conspired with other enemies of the republic to benefit themselves at the expense of White Christian Americans.

According to Ezekiel (1995), the leaders of White supremacist organizations are motivated less by sheer hate than by a burning desire to assume a position of power and to be important in the eyes of others. Their followers are recruited from the ranks of marginalized and alienated Americans, many poorly educated and financially troubled, who are searching for a sense of belonging that they never had at home, but they find readily available in organized hate (Langer, 1990).

Expanding the Influence of Organized Hate

At the same time, marginality and alienation do not always depend on impoverishment. Although most White supremacists are from working-class backgrounds, there are also some who seem to be well-educated and wealthy. One of the most tragic examples of the appeal of racism and anti-Semitism to an economically advantaged White supremacist can be found in the July 1999 three-day rampage of 21-year-old Benjamin Smith, in which the Indiana University student murdered a Korean graduate student on his campus and a Black basketball coach at Northwestern University. He also fired bullets at a group of Orthodox Jews, injuring six of them before taking his own life.

Smith, whose father was a physician, grew up in an affluent suburb northwest of Chicago. His mentor was, however, not his father, but 27-year-old Matthew Hale, the son of a police officer. He is a law-school graduate from East Peoria who, based on his racist beliefs and practices, was denied the privilege of practicing law by the state of Illinois. In his role as head of the White supremacist group World Church of the Creator (now known as the Creativity Movement), Hale was able to express his racist views to a group of followers who were eager to hear them. Before serving a lengthy prison sentence for conspiring to murder a judge, Hale had been in contact with Smith for several days prior to the young man's murderous rampage through Illinois and Indiana and considered Smith a martyr and a friend. Some questioned whether Hale had inspired Smith's killing spree.

Hale also preached Ra-Ho-Wa— the inevitability of a racial holy war from which Whites would ultimately emerge the winners. He despised Jews, Blacks, Latinos, and Asians, considering them to be subhumans at the same level as animals. He also argued that Christianity was merely a tool of deception used by power-hungry Jews to nurture a mindset that would enable them to take over the world. Smith was reportedly furious when he learned that the state of Illinois had denied Hale's bid to practice law. This may have been the catalyst that initiated his killing spree.

Peer pressure may also have been a factor. Smith's girlfriend, 20-year-old Christine Weiss, was also a member of Hale's World Church of the Creator. Like her boyfriend, Weiss had grown up in a wealthy Chicago suburb. She had played soccer and classical music for 11 years and had attended the same high school as Smith, one of the best in the country. Then, Weiss learned on the Internet about World Church of the Creator and Matthew Hale. After graduating from high school, she disavowed her Episcopalian roots and joined up. She now talks about preparing for the racial holy war espoused by Hale and about caring only for "her own kind"—the White people of the world (CNN, 2000).

The Internet and its thousands of hate Web sites give to hatemongers a degree of influence well beyond their small numbers. Thanks to the Internet, Mat Hale's message of hate has reached thousands of young people around the country who may have racist and anti-Semitic feelings and are thrilled to learn that they are not alone in these beliefs.

According to former racist Tom Leyden, the Internet is probably the best thing ever to happen to the White supremacist movement. Any child with a computer can access hundreds of hate Web sites, including that of Matthew Hale's organization. In fact, 6-year-olds can even visit the Web site called World Church of the Creator for Kids, where they can find a crossword puzzle to solve and a White power coloring book to download.

Leyden should know about hate. He preaches tolerance for the Simon Wiesenthal Center in Los Angeles, but he's not Jewish. For 15 years, he was a neo-Nazi skinhead whose body was covered with racist and anti-Semitic tattoos. In his younger days, when he wasn't in jail, Leyden was in the streets, fighting, attacking, and beating up people he considered to be his enemies.

Leyden later married another White supremacist. But when he had children, he felt it was time to make a profound change in his life. There was no way, he reasoned, that he was going to raise his sons in the image of the Nazi movement. There was no way that he was going to contribute to the making of the next generation of hatemongers. Now, he works for the other side, seeking to make up for the time he lost in his early years that was filled with hate and prejudice.

Leyden's reference to the Internet should not be taken lightly. As he suggested in a CNN (2000) interview with correspondent Art Harris, there are youngsters in small towns and big cities around the country who feel alone in their racism. They don't have friends; they have trouble getting along with their peers. But when they boot up their computers and log onto the Internet, they've got good friends literally around the world who love them and who agree with their racist views.

Because of the Internet, hate Web sites originating in the United States have also had a powerful impact on youngsters in other countries where the restrictions on hate are more rigorously applied. According to German law, for example, the dissemination of Nazi propaganda is strictly forbidden. Yet, German laws banning hate on the Internet have been easily circumvented by the spread of Web sites in the United States operated by neo-Nazi extremists and accessible in the German language to German youths. Protected by the First Amendment to the Constitution, U.S. sites offer propaganda, insignias, music, and computer games that have been officially outlawed from German society but are nevertheless within easy reach of German youths. There are many computer hate games available from American sources, including Concentration Camp Manager, an extremely popular game among German teenagers in which players choose who lives and who dies in the gas chambers. Other computer games have been modified by American Nazis who add an element of hate to what would otherwise be an innocuous form of high tech entertainment. In the game Grouse Hunt, for example, the virtual pheasants to be shot were replaced by yamulkes (Jewish prayer caps) and Stars of David. According to a German Interior Ministry estimate, the number of Nazi sites outside Germany that are directed at German citizens has recently soared (Finn, 2000).

DABBLERS

For hardened hatemongers, bigotry becomes the basis for a full-time preoccupation, if not a career. They join an organization that espouses racism or other forms of prejudice. They completely limit their friendships to those who hold their bigoted beliefs. And they practice what they preach by waging a continuing campaign of intimidation against the "outsiders" they despise.

Getting a Thrill

Yet, in everyday life, not all hate incidents are so clearly hate-filled. Certain individuals *dabble* in bigotry. They convert their prejudices into behavior, but only on a part-time basis as a hobby, for example, by going out on a Saturday night with their buddies to assault someone, to burn a cross, or to spray-paint graffiti. Dabblers are typically young people, usually groups of teenage boys or young adults who aren't getting along at home, in school, or on the job. They may hate themselves as much as they hate their victims. But in committing a hate crime, they gain what seems to be missing from their lives. They feel superior to the extent that they make their victim feel inferior. They feel important by their actions in reducing their enemies to the status of garbage. Moreover, many hate attacks directed against Blacks, gays, Latinos, Asians, and Jews are committed by dabblers who gain "bragging rights" with their friends at the same time that they fill their idle hours with excitement.

Not all of those who band together to bash vulnerable victims are responsible for instigating an attack. Indeed, in any group of dabblers, there is usually a leader who has sadistic tendencies that he is eager to satisfy by making life miserable for the enemy. In addition, there are usually at least a few "fellow travelers" who go along with their friends, so as to avoid being rejected (Watts, 1997). In questioning college students in Boston, for example, I identified some who had not verbalized an objection when their friend threatened to do harm to a member of another group. One young Asian woman remarked,

> A friend of mine threatened someone else who was of a rival gang. My friend was Asian and was racially biased against other races, but would only threaten to hurt those who were in gangs. I was shocked that he would say that and quietly hoped he wouldn't follow through on the threat.

The phenomenon of the fellow traveler may have applied very neatly to a recent hate crime involving a group of eight Southern California teenagers who brutally attacked five elderly Latino nursery workers, apparently just for the fun of it. Bored and unable to think of any legal forms of entertainment to amuse themselves, the youngsters drove slowly through the darkened streets of the city, searching for a little excitement. Finally, they came upon the Latino nursery workers. At first, the teenagers only shouted ethnic slurs at the Latinos from their passing car. Then, five of the boys got out of the car and began shooting the workers with pellet guns and beating them with rocks. All the while, three of the teenagers participated minimally in the attack, seated uncomfortably in the car where they talked together in hushed tones about being scared and about how things were getting out of control. One of them reluctantly retrieved ammunition to re-arm one of the teenager's pellet guns, but apparently he never directly participated in the attack (Roth, 2001).

Struggling with a high unemployment rate and widespread resentment toward Jews and foreigners, the former East Germany has recently had more than its share of thrill hate attacks. Some of them deadly. In 1989–1990, just prior to unification of east and west, there were fewer than 200 acts of hate aimed at foreigners, Jews, and political opponents; most of these were perpetrated by German adults who were linked to neo-Nazi hate groups.

Throughout the 1990s and into the twenty-first century, however, as the unemployment rate grew and immigration increased, the number of violent attacks almost quadrupled. In 2004 alone, there were 776 cases of racial or ethnic assaults—mostly beatings, attempted murders, and arson attacks—in German cities and towns. From the fall of the Berlin

Wall to the present, neo-Nazis have murdered more than 100 foreigners, according to reports in the German press (Nickerson, 2006).

Even the personal characteristics of activist bigots changed after unification. During the 1980s, most of the racist demonstrators were older and connected with organized neo-Nazi groups. By contrast, after unification, the vast majority of attackers were under the age of 20—teenagers who were driven more by personal misery than by political ideology. Fewer had ties to organized hate groups or were in touch with Nazi beliefs. Like their counterparts in the United States, the German bigots tended to be alienated and marginalized young people who saw little hope for the future and blamed refugees, Jews, and guest workers for all of their woes (Watts, 1997).

Some episodes of hate violence turned particularly brutal. In June 2000, three young racist teenagers in the city of Dessau missed the last train back to their hometown of Bitterfeld and, being bored, decided to go out and get drunk. Two were high-school dropouts; one was out of work. All of them enjoyed listening to the lyrics of anti-Semitic violent music such as "Auschwitz, Dachau, Buchenwald, we're going to bump off the Jews again" and "Our faces are full of hatred. We love violence" (Leparmentier, 2000).

Shortly after midnight, having been thrown out of the train station where they had been drinking heavily, the trio staggered through the streets of Dessau and into a local park, where they encountered Alberto Adriano, a 39-year-old Black man of Mozambican descent. He had come to the town of Dessau 12 years earlier and was married to a German woman. Shouting "filthy nigger, get out of our country," the three bigoted teenagers knocked down their victim and repeatedly hit and kicked him in the head, even as he lay helplessly on the ground and appeared to be dead. Then, to humiliate Adriano, the three young men tore off his clothes so that he was left lying in the park with nothing on except his socks and shoes. Their sadism suggests strongly that the three young racists in hate were motivated more by a profound psychological need than any political end.

In August 2000, a judge handed down sentences to the trio for the brutal murder of Alberto Adriano. The two 16-year-olds received nine years in prison; their 24-year-old companion received a life sentence. When asked by the judge what he had against foreigners, one of the 16-year-old defendants replied simply, "I hate niggers."

Not unlike the killers of Alberto Adriano in Germany, many dabblers in countries around the world suffer from marginality based on economic and/or educational disadvantage. Some may come from wealthy families, but nevertheless they feel a profound sense of social marginality in relation to their families or peers. In the United States anxious advocates of nativism envision huddled masses of impoverished, uneducated, disease-ridden criminals who sneak across our porous borders to steal jobs and murder our citizens.

The massacre at Columbine High School in Littleton, Colorado, served to alert us to the possibility that alienation leading to hate can occur in even upper-middle-class communities. Columbine's two youthful mass murderers, Dylan Klebold and Eric Harris, apparently did not suffer in any economic sense. Both were college bound and apparently had bright futures in the job market. But they were regarded by their classmates as geeks or nerds, they were bullied and belittled by the popular students at Columbine High, and they felt a profound sense of rejection. As a result, they banned together with other outcasts who respected and admired Adolph Hitler (indeed, Klebold and Harris timed their mass murder so that it occurred on Hitler's birthday). Moreover, they adopted symbols of power and hate in images of evil, swastikas, the trenchcoat Mafia, and gothic incivility. It is no coincidence that their first victim was one of the few Black students at Columbine High—a popular student athlete.

Typically, dabblers do not limit their attacks to any specific group. The interesting thing theoretically is that a dabbler who hates someone because he or she is Black is also likely to hate someone who is Latino or gay or Asian or Jewish or disabled (Sniderman and Piazza, 1993). This lack of specialization in the selection of a victim probably reflects the dabbler's psychological need to feel good about himself at somebody else's expense. Our culture supplies the dabbler with a range of enemies who would be appropriate to vandalize, bash, threaten, intimidate, or assault. He makes his selection from this range of cultural villains based on what is convenient at the time.

Being Defensive

Not all dabblers are looking for just a thrill. According to Levin and McDevitt (1995a), a second type of dabbler is motivated to commit hate crimes that are believed to be *defensive*. Such attacks are typically precipitated by a threatening episode, for example, a gay rights parade, Blacks moving into a previously all-White neighborhood, a terrorist attack by Muslim extremists, or the first Latino or Asian student on a campus. Failing to elicit the desired response (e.g., the immediate withdrawal of a Latino family from a previously all-White neighborhood), there may be an escalation of violence. A verbal attack by phone may become a personal visit with a firearm; a hate crime that begins as vandalism may turn more deadly.

Research conducted by the *Chicago Reporter* (Gordon, 1997) suggests that Chicago-area suburbs with growing minority populations have experienced increasing numbers of hate offenses against Blacks and Latinos. In many previously all-White suburban communities, minorities have reached a critical mass, causing White residents to feel threatened by the influx of newcomers. This seems to be the point at which hate crimes escalate.

Those who argue that hate crimes increased through the 1980s and 1990s note also that intergroup competition rose as well during this period (Olzak et al., 1996). Whether or not economically based, growing threats to the advantaged majority group since the early 1980s may have inspired a rising tide of hate incidents directed against members of challenging groups. Over the past 20 years or so, there have been dramatic increases in interfaith and interrace dating and marriage; migration especially from Latin America and Asia; newly integrated neighborhoods, schools, college dormitories, and workplaces; and gay men and lesbians coming out (and, in many cases, organizing on behalf of their shared interests). Donald Green and his associates (1997) have shown that hate crimes occur most frequently in "defended" White neighborhoods, that is, in predominantly White areas that have experienced an in-migration of minorities. Broadening Green's concept a bit, I suggest that dabblers in hate may defend any aspect of their lives they feel especially entitled to hold—not only their neighborhood, but their campus, their dormitory, their office, or their social relationships.

The concept of defended neighborhood is illustrated by a hate crime that occurred in Salt Lake City on the Saturday evening before Labor Day in September 1998. A 25-year-old man, Michael Magleby, and his 15-year-old accomplice snuck onto the lawn of a modest single-family house. Asleep in their home were Ron Henry, who is Black, his wife, who is White, and their 12-year-old son. Awakened by a sudden noise outside, the three ran to a window and watched as a cross burned brightly on their lawn.

As a consultant for the prosecution, I was able to interview Ron Henry in the course of Magleby's trial. It was clear to me that Ron understood the symbolism of the burning cross all too well. It was intended to intimidate him, to threaten him with violence, to scare him into leaving the neighborhood. For two weeks afterwards, Ron was frightened enough to install a security system in his home. He began carrying a baseball bat whenever he and his son took walks around the neighborhood. He considered leaving the area.

Trial evidence confirmed that Ron Henry's fear was not misplaced. Michael Magleby was known to visit hate Web sites, collect racist propaganda, read White supremacist novels such as *The Turner Diaries,* and listen to White power CDs including the racist lyrics of Skrewdriver. Just before he was convicted in federal court, the prosecuting attorney identified Magleby's motive. He argued that only a racist would even think of burning a cross on the lawn of a Black. It was clear, he said, that the defendant wanted Henry out of the area, and the burning cross was meant to convey a message to that effect (Rayburn, 1999).

The prevalence of defensive hate crimes has historically risen and fallen, depending on the particular economic circumstances of the times. During periods of economic downturn in the 1980s and 1990s, for example, Asian Americans often became the targets of hate. Just as Jews had been blamed for Germany's economic woes during the Nazi era, Asians were held responsible for America's declining position in the global economy. In 1982, during the deepest recession since World War II, a Chinese American man, celebrating just prior to his wedding day, was killed by two recently out-of-work automobile employees in Detroit who blamed the Japanese for their financial problems and failed to distinguish Chinese from Japanese or Asian Americans from Asians (Levin and McDevitt, 2002).

Ten years later, just as an epidemic of corporate downsizing hit the American economy, the Los Angeles office of the Japanese American Citizens League received a bomb threat in which the caller warned, "I'll show you a year of remembrance, you dirty Japs. What we remember is Pearl Harbor." During the same period, an Asian American from Sacramento was stabbed to death by someone who sought to "defend our country" from the onslaught of Asian newcomers (Ancheta, 1998, p. 74).

In a 1992 study of hate crimes reported to the Boston police, it was found that Asians and Latinos were the two groups at greatest risk for victimization. These are the "new kids on the block," the newcomers who are seen as threatening the economic well-being of groups of Americans who have been here longer and who now feel they must protect their stake in the country (Levin and McDevitt, 1993, 1995a; McDevitt, et al., 2002).

According to the most recent data released by the U.S. Census Bureau, such "defensive" hate attacks might be expected to increase over the next several years. In the 2000 census, the number of Latinos soared to the point where they have now surpassed Black Americans to become the largest minority group in the nation. More specifically, Latinos represented 6.4 percent of the total population in 1980; by the year 2000, they were 12.5 percent (Rodriguez, 2001). Similarly, the Asian population grew by leaps and bounds, especially in and around large cities. In New Jersey, for example, there was a 94 percent increase. In Pennsylvania, the Asian population grew by 83 percent (Armas, 2001).

Getting Even

The growing concern about terrorism coming from radical elements of Islam has created a new wrinkle in the complexion of intergroup relations among America's Muslims, Christians, and Jews. In the aftermath of 9-11, there was an escalation in defensive hate crimes committed against Arabs and Muslims in the United States. Operating on the basis of diffuse anger and a profound sense of frustration, some Americans decided to carry out vigilante actions against individuals whom they regarded as the disloyal supporters of anti-American terror. Thus, Middle Easterners and

Muslims (as well as individuals who only looked like Middle Easterners or Muslims) were vulnerable to attack, regardless of their personal loyalties and beliefs. The perpetrators never stopped to determine the unique characteristics of those singled out for abuse and punishment. A foreign accent, dark skin, a veil or a turban made all the difference.

On occasion, hate crimes perpetrated by the members of one group trigger a *retaliatory* strike by members of the victims' group. In such a case, the victims of hate offenses become the perpetrators; they seek revenge for the injustices they have suffered. Their targets are typically selected on a random basis, so that each and every member of a group is a potential victim. A retaliatory hate crime may have occurred on March 4, 2006, when Mohammed Reza Taheri-azar, a 22-year-old native of Iran who had spent most of his life in the United States, allegedly drove his rented sport utility vehicle through a crowded gathering place on the campus of the University of North Carolina, where he had recently graduated. Six students, including a visiting scholar on campus, were slightly injured. According to FBI sources, Taheri-azar indicated that his motive was to avenge the shoddy treatment of Muslims around the world (Dalesio, 2006).

On March 10, Taheri-azar sent the following letter from Central Prison in Raleigh to a reporter at the local ABC-TV affiliate:

> Allah gives permission in the Koran for the followers of Allah to attack those who have raged war against them, with the expectation of eternal paradise in case of martyrdom and/or living one's life in obedience of all of Allah's commandments found throughout the Koran's 114 chapters . . .
>
> The U.S. government is responsible for the deaths of and the torture of countless followers of Allah, my brothers and sisters. My attack on Americans at UNC-CH on March 3rd was in retaliation for similar attacks orchestrated by the U.S. government on my fellow followers of Allah in Iraq, Afghanistan, Palestine, Saudi Arabia, and other Islamic territories. (Taheri-azar, 2006; ABC11tv.com, 2006)

Most defensive and retaliatory hate crimes in the United States and England take the form of vandalism, intimidation, and simple assault (Levin and McDevitt, 2002; Iganski, Kielinger, and Paterson, 2005). On occasion, however, the defensive aim of an attacker is transformed into a *mission*. The hatemonger is no longer satisfied just to remove one Black family from the neighborhood. Now he dedicates himself to eliminating as many Black Americans as possible. In some cases, the hatemonger takes his defensive stance to a new and more deadly level. He commits a pre-emptive strike against the enemy.

Shortly after midnight on February 2, 2006, 18-year-old Jacob Robida walked into Puzzles Lounge, a popular gay gathering place in the city of New Bedford, Massachusetts, 50 miles south of Boston, and ordered a drink at the bar. Then, after having one more shot of whiskey, he walked to the back of the room near a pool table and took a hatchet from his black trenchcoat. Two men were able to grab the hatchet from the assailant's hands, but not before Robida had slashed both of them in the face. He then pulled out a 9 mm pistol and shot a third man in the stomach. Next, he put the gun to his own head and pulled the trigger. When it failed to fire, Robida ran out the front door of Puzzles Lounge and into the night.

Robida's rampage had just begun. After escaping from the gay bar where he left three men seriously wounded, he drove to Charleston, West Virginia, and picked up 33-year-old Jennifer Bailey, a woman with whom he had previously lived. The couple drove to Gassville, Arkansas, where Robida confronted police officer James Sell, who had asked him to pull over to the side of the road in a routine traffic stop. Robida first gunned down Sell, then shot to death his female companion. He finally turned the gun on himself, taking his own life as the police closed in on him (Southern Poverty Law Center, 2006).

It was no coincidence that Robida had initiated his rampage by targeting gays. The first thing he had asked the bartender before slashing and shooting patrons was "Is this a gay bar?" According to those who knew him well, he hated gays and lesbians, but he also despised Blacks and Jews. His Web site on MySpace.com contained a photograph of himself wielding a firearm with a swastika in the background. His bedroom walls were covered with anti-Semitic writings and swastikas. Robida had an extensive collection of Nazi memorabilia, including books about the Third Reich, Nazi flags, and a sword. Among his books was a copy of *The Turner Diaries*, a neo-Nazi novel that many believe had inspired Timothy McVeigh's 1995 massacre in Oklahoma City (CBS4Boston, 2006).

SYMPATHIZERS

Millions of Americans may not be active hatemongers or even dabblers, but they agree in principle with those who are. Such "timid bigots" can be regarded as *sympathizers*—their prejudiced attitudes are generally at a verbal level only (Merton, 1957). They may repeat a joke to their like-minded associates and that is as far as they are willing to go, but their voices give encouragement and comfort to those who express their hatred in discrimination or violence. Moreover, because of their refusal to cooperate with those who seek to bring bigots to justice, sympathizers also share responsibility for the acts that their sympathetic stance makes possible.

The sympathy for bigotry is not always clear-cut or consistent. This was indicated by a college student in the Boston area whom I recently questioned about her prejudices. She was a White woman who confessed having been told a joke that referred to another race in a derogatory way. When asked how she responded to the bigoted joke, she answered

It was humorous. However, this doesn't necessarily mean I agree with using the terms, because I don't (not in a serious manner). I thought the joke was funny and remembered it for my repertoire of good jokes that I tell other people who share my ideas about members of that group.

Behind Closed Doors

Though hardly represented among violent bigots, sympathizers play an especially important role in perpetuating institutionalized forms of discrimination against underrepresented groups in society. In the atmosphere of an executive boardroom, a real estate agency, or a university admissions office, verbal bigotry may be just what it takes to stifle the ambitions of individuals who seek jobs, homes, or a place in the classroom. The individual hatred of powerful decision-makers can easily be transformed into company policy.

This was seen when it was disclosed that in 1994 certain Texaco directors, while meeting together to formulate company policy concerning racial discrimination, had been caught on tape voicing racist feelings about their Black employees. Using a metaphor to discuss with sarcasm the failure of Black workers to be promoted, one director asked, "Isn't it funny how the Black jelly beans seem to get stuck to the bottom of the bag?" Another complained, "I'm still having trouble with Hanukkah. Now we have Kwanzaa."

Some observers connected directors' attitudes with the fact that tiny numbers of Black workers had attained executive positions in the Texaco hierarchy. Indeed, although 22 percent of its employees were Black, Texaco had no Black heads of departments or vice-presidents. No Blacks sat on its board of directors (White, 1996).

An Eliminationist Anti-Semitism

Given the appropriate conditions, some sympathizers can be moved to dabble in bigotry or even to become hatemongers. According to Goldhagen (1996), tens of thousands of German citizens during the Nazi era of the 1930s, reacting to Hitler's interpretation of a terrible economic situation, translated their sympathy for anti-Semitism into mass murder.

At the Nuremberg War Crimes Trials, defendants sought unsuccessfully to elude responsibility for their participation in the Nazi slaughter by arguing they had been mesmerized into obeying the orders of a charismatic Adolph Hitler. Rather than admit that they approved of what he represented, they spoke instead of Hitler's domineering presence, his irresistible magnetism, his ability to cast a hypnotic spell. Their defense was meant to let them off the hook: "No Hitler, no Holocaust" (Weiss, 1996).

According to Weiss (1996), even the most powerful orators cannot possibly convert those who have not already bought into their ideas. Radical demagogues have the capacity to confirm but not to convince. It was not Hitler's style so much as the substance of his rhetoric that persuaded hundreds of thousands of German citizens to participate in, or at the very least not to oppose, the massacre of Jews.

Of course, there may be some limited circumstances, for example, among prisoners of war, where the control over an individual is absolute or complete. Under such conditions, it may actually be appropriate to speak in terms of "brainwashing," "mind control," or "thought reform" (Lifton, 1961). But in most of the circumstances of everyday life, individuals possess an element of free will that can only be manipulated so much. The most authoritarian and charismatic leader cannot completely undermine individual autonomy and voluntarism. In fact, it is pure myth to suggest that the members of a society collectively lack any power to resist while under the spell of a madman. Even extremely vulnerable individuals possess an "active self" that severely limits the power of the most persuasive leader to mold or shape the behavior and beliefs of his followers (Tabor and Gallagher, 1995).

Cultural Hate

It would be comforting if we were able to characterize hate and prejudice as deviant, irrational, and pathological behavior—as an aspect of the domain of a few "crazies" on the fringe of society whose psychosis is in urgent need of treatment by psychotherapy, psychotropic medications, or both. Unfortunately, hate hardly depends for its existence on individual pathology or abnormal psychology. Nor is it a form of deviance from the point of view of mainstream society. Even if the admission of being prejudiced is unacceptable, hate itself is instead normal, rational, and conventional. It is part of the culture—the way of life—of the society in which it exists, appealing typically to the most conventional and traditional of its members (Westie, 1964; Feagin and Vera, 1995; Barnett, 1999).

Even in such an extreme set of circumstances as the atrocities committed under Nazism, genocide was carried out and encouraged not by ideological fanatics and schizophrenics but by ordinary citizens. Even the perpetrators were normal by conventional mental health standards. The power of Nazism was indeed strong, but it hardly prevented most ordinary citizens from making ethical decisions and functioning in a normal way (Barnett, 1999; Browning, 1992). For example, Polish authorities suggested for decades that the Nazis had been responsible for a 1941 massacre of the Jewish residents of the town of Jedwabne. New evidence argued that it was not Nazi soldiers but ordinary Polish farmers who herded 1600 of their Jewish neighbors into a barn and set it on fire (Stylinski, 2001).

Where it is cultural, sympathy for a particular hatred may become a widely shared and enduring element in the normal state of affairs of a group of people. Even more important, the prejudice may become systematically organized to reward individuals who are bigoted and cruel and to punish those individuals who are caring and respectful of differences (Katz, 1993). In such circumstances, tolerance for group differences may actually be regarded as rebellious behavior and those who openly express tolerance may be viewed as rebels.

Sympathizers draw their hate from the culture, developing it from an early age. As a cultural phenomenon, racism is as American as apple pie. It has been around for centuries and is learned by every generation in the same way that our most cherished cultural values have been acquired: around the dinner table; through books and television programs; from teachers, friends, and relatives (Levin and Levin, 1982).

In the American experience, White racism has a long and deep cultural history, being traceable back centuries to the impetus in the New World for enslaving large numbers of Africans rather than White Europeans. Racism can therefore be seen not as a conscious conspiracy of powerful people or the delusional thinking of a few radical bigots. Rather, it is an important, if largely unconscious, aspect of America's historical experience and of our shared cultural order, arising from the taken-for-granted assumptions that Americans learn to make about themselves and others (Kovel, 1971; Lawrence, 1987; Smith, 1995).

Stereotyping also seems to have a cultural basis that is dependent on the cognitive development of an individual. As a result, the particular cultural images of a group of people may not be accepted, or even understood, by a child until long after she has already developed an intense hatred toward its members.

Later on, education seems to be effective in reducing stereotyped thinking. In addition, legislation can, within limits, reduce discriminatory behavior. Yet, the emotional component of hate may persevere over the course of a lifetime, regardless of attempts to modify it. Beginning so early in life, hate may become a passion for the individual who acquires it, being much harder to modify than stereotypes or the tendency to discriminate (Levin and Levin, 1982).

The cultural element of hate can be seen in its amazing ability to sweep across broad areas of a nation. Individuals separated by region, age, social class, and ethnic background all tend to share roughly the same stereotyped images of various groups. In the United States, for example, some degree of anti-Black, anti-Asian, and anti-Latino racism can be found among substantial segments of Americans—males and females, young and old, rich and poor—from New York to California, from North Dakota to Texas.

Similarly, in Nazi Germany, Hitler's condemnation of the Jews reflected not only his personal opinion, but also the beliefs of hundreds of thousands of German and Austrian citizens. While the police looked on approvingly, university students joined together to beat and batter their

Jewish classmates. Faculty members and students voiced demands to rid the universities of Jews and cosponsored lectures on "the Jewish problem." Because of their genuine conviction, thousands of German soldiers and police helped to murder Jews. Civil service bureaucrats aided in doing the paperwork to expedite carrying out Hitler's extermination program. Many important business, banking, and industrial firms cooperated in the task of enslaving and murdering Jewish citizens. Thousands of German physicians cooperated in sterilizing or eliminating the "undesirables." Finally, whereas the church in other European countries denounced racist anti-Semitism, Germany's religious leaders (both Catholic and Protestant) failed to protest the final solution (Weiss, 1996).

At the cultural level, the emotional character of racial or religious hatred is reflected collectively in laws and norms that prohibit intimate contact between different groups of people. In the Deep South, Jim Crow laws created separate public facilities: "colored" and "White" restrooms, waiting rooms, water fountains, and sections on public buses. In the South African version of apartheid, Blacks were similarly restricted to living in segregated communities and could work among Whites only under the strictest supervision.

In Nazi Germany, the same sort of enduring sympathy for hate might be found among citizens concerning anti-Semitism. In explaining the particular stronghold of Hitler's "final solution," Goldhagen (1996) has argued that an "eliminationist anti-Semitism" was a longstanding feature of German culture that dated back centuries. The majority of ordinary German citizens believed that the Jews, ostensibly being responsible for all of their country's economic woes, had to be eliminated at any cost. Thus, rather than some dark and repulsive secret, gruesome stories about the Nazi's brutal anti-Jewish policies—the death camps, gas chambers, hideous experiments, and mass murders—were told and retold proudly across the land to ordinary German citizens who were eager to hear them.

Nazi anti-Semitism was located at the end of a continuum of cultural bigotry that seems to have helped determine the fate of Jews not only in Germany but in other European countries as well. Nations such as Poland and Hungary, which had a longstanding tradition of anti-Semitic attitudes and behavior, were also nations in which a large proportion of Jews was murdered; countries such as Denmark, Belgium, and Bulgaria where a tradition of tolerance and respect for religious diversity was strong were also countries where a relatively sizable proportion of Jews survived (Fein, 1979).

Culture Transcends Generations

At precisely the same time in the 1800s when it was on the decline in other western European countries, anti-Semitism increased rapidly among the populations of Germany and Austria. By the 1890s, anti-Jewish feelings had gained widespread acceptance throughout the same generation that would later bring Hitler to power. Nazism was initially only one of the political movements to espouse anti-Semitic policies. In 1919, political parties across the ideological spectrum merged to fight a more effective battle against the "rule of the Jews." Huge amounts of anti-Jewish political propaganda were disseminated to the masses (Weiss, 1996).

Moreover, even long after Hitler's death and the defeat of the Nazi movement during World War II, anti-Semitism continued to thrive and prosper. An analysis of anti-Jewish attitudes in eastern and western Germany found that strong anti-Semitism remained in western Germany even after "four decades of re-education . . . and a nearly total taboo on public expressions of anti-Semitism" (Watts, 1997, p. 219). A survey of German youngsters recently found that more than a third believe that Hitler's regime had "a good side" and nearly 40 percent said that Nazism had its good points. In the former East Germany, where the economy continues to be shaky, 15 percent of all 14- to 16-year-old respondents thought that Nazism was a good idea (Helm, 2001).

On the other side of the racial ledger, it is also no coincidence that the country of Bulgaria, whose people actively defied Hitler to a greater extent than any other Nazi-allied country, has remained at peace with itself, despite an unemployment rate varying between 13 and 15 percent and an ethnic mix that resembles that of its next-door neighbor, the former Yugoslavia. Just like its opposite, respect for differences often also has a cultural component.

SPECTATORS

As we have seen, Daniel Goldhagen (1996) proposed that the specifically German form of anti-Semitism that he labels "eliminationist" in its objective was responsible for the mass extermination of Jews under Hitler. Taking a cultural viewpoint, Goldhagen argued that German anti-Semitism during the 1930s was deeply rooted in German history, finding its origins in a longstanding desire among German citizens for the liquidation of their Jewish neighbors, dating back to the nineteenth century, if not earlier. Thus, the mass murder of German Jews under the Nazi regime involved more than a million "willing executioners." These were average German citizens who actively participated in the slaughter or who, at the very least, regarded the mass extermination of Jews as necessary for the survival of German society. Those who did the killing hardly tried to conceal their deadly jobs from family and friends; instead, they bragged and joked about their role in death camps to an eager audience of ordinary citizens.

The Failure to Act

But Goldhagen has been widely criticized for relying so heavily on German national character and culture as an explanation for the Nazi holocaust (see Shandley, 1998). Most other scholars agree with Goldhagen that anti-Semitism was a predisposing factor, but not the only one nor perhaps even the most important. Other European countries, not just Germany, had virulent forms of anti-Semitism. And many Germans, although perhaps indifferent to the plight of Jews, were hardly enthusiastic in their support of the Nazi program.

Looking at the rise of anti-Jewish policies and practices across nations, Brustein and King (in press) have suggested that cultural bigotry cannot by itself adequately explain the escalation of anti-Semitic practices in western societies just prior to the Nazi Holocaust or variations in anti-Semitic practices across countries and time. The rise in anti-Semitism between 1879 and 1939 varied significantly depending on the extent to which Jews were perceived as a threat to non-Jews. In five countries—Germany, Romania, Great Britain, Italy, and France—anti-Semitism grew when the nation's level of prosperity deteriorated and the level of immigration of eastern European Jews increased.

This was certainly the case in Nazi Germany. There were important situational and economic factors in the German experience. For example, the breadth and depth of inflation in its economy, the charismatic leadership of the Third Reich, and the vulnerable status of Germany after World War I may have contributed significantly to the appeal of eliminationist thinking. Moreover, although the massacre of Jews was at a genocidal level, many other groups (gypsies, elders, eastern Europeans, gays, and people with disabilities) also suffered tremendous losses.

When questioned about their cooperation with the Nazi movement, many German citizens characterized themselves as "little people" who were powerless to influence the course of Hitler's final solution. What they failed to acknowledge, however, was that millions of ordinary people throughout Germany gave their support, whether active or inactive, to Nazism. Of their own free will, many joined the Nazi party, worked to enact its policies, and encouraged their own husbands and sons to fight for the Fatherland (Katz, 1993).

In fact, many Germans were motivated to acquiesce less by cultural anti-Semitism than by self-interest. Some could not muster the courage; others took a practical path that they felt would be more beneficial. The Nazis never gained more than 37 percent of the vote in a free election. For a relatively few German citizens during the 1930s, eliminating Jews was a top priority; for the largest part of the German population, however, it was not (Browning, 1992). Indeed, there seemed to be less active support and more passive acceptance of Nazi policies borne of indifference, discomfort at the thought of the fate of German Jews, and fear of the Nazi leaders (Barnett, 1999).

As suggested by Elie Wiesel (1977), apathy is actually a version of complicity that facilitates the spread of hatred and bigotry. Although not acting out of an eliminationist anti-Semitism, most German citizens nevertheless accepted legal, economic, and political measures that would eventually drive Jews from Germany and into death camps. They supported measures carried out in an orderly and a legal manner such as those removing Jews from public positions in 1933, socially isolating Jews in 1935, and confiscating their property in 1938. The same German citizens who supported the legal persecution of Jews were opposed to violent anti-Semitism, for example, the boycott of 1933, the collective vandalism of 1935, and the Kristallnacht bloodletting of 1938 (Browning, 1992). When it came to the fate of the Jews, however, German citizens seemed to be increasingly apathetic. The indifference of "ordinary Germans" gave the Nazi regime exactly what it needed, the freedom to proceed toward a "final solution" (Browning, 1992).

During the 1930s, spectatorship was alive and well in German life. Very few Germans were willing to stand and be counted in opposition to the removal and massacre of Jews. Aside from cultural considerations, there were severe economic exigencies to which Hitler had promised an effective response. There were new laws allowing the persecution of Jews that would have to be violated. And there was always the threat of being discovered, turned in, and treated as a traitor (Staub, 1989).

During the Nazi era, moreover, many otherwise decent German citizens benefitted in a material sense from the confiscation of Jewish property (Browning, 1992). Personal belongings and furniture were auctioned to the highest bidder, and tens of thousands of Jewish apartments were taken over. In addition, the expulsion of Jews from prestigious or lucrative occupations seriously reduced the competition for well-paying and high-status jobs. On the other side, citizens of Germany and Nazi-occupied European countries who aided Jews by concealing them from German soldiers exposed themselves to the possibility of paying the ultimate price. In one Ukranian village, for example, an entire family— including husband, wife, and three children—were shot to death for sheltering a Jewish woman (Hilberg, 1992).

The concept of the spectator can be expanded well beyond individual citizens to characterize companies, religious groups, banks, and entire countries whose decision-makers respond to bigotry with a form of passive acceptance that is tantamount to complicity. Hitler's regime was aided and abetted in moving toward its final solution by countries around the world that refused to admit Jews who were otherwise on their way to death camps, by church leaders who refused to condemn Nazism, by political leaders outside Germany who allied themselves with the Third Reich, and by western companies that supplied Hitler's subordinates with machines needed to increase the efficiency of the process for identifying, transporting, and exterminating Jews and other victims of the Nazis.

Middleman Minorities

The visibility of Jews in the social structure of Germany during the 1930s also gave them special vulnerability. During the Nazi period, German Jews represented only one half of one percent of the country's population. But they were disproportionately located in middle- and upper-middle-class occupations—the butcher down the block, the doctor on the next street, the teacher at the local school, the reporter at the town's newspaper. Jewish wealth, therefore, tended to be of the "in your face" variety, a constant reminder to impoverished Germans that many of their Jewish neighbors were economically better off than they were. In this sense, German Jews can be regarded as a "middleman minority."

According to Beller (1997), German anti-Semitism was in part a consequence of the middleman role of Jewish citizens in German and Austrian society. He focuses particularly on the city of Vienna, where early on anti-Jewish policies and practices took hold. In the aftermath of the crash of 1873, many Austrians lost confidence in liberal political and social policies to produce prosperity for the masses. Because of restrictions on their educational and occupational opportunities, Vienna's Jews remained a distinct and separate socioeconomic community that was disproportionately represented in finance and commerce and the professions considered to be "liberal." Their friendships, alliances, and marriage partners were primarily confined to other Jews. And even though there may have been some "spatial mingling" in apartment blocks and schools, Jews kept pretty much to Jews and Christians kept pretty much to Christians.

Viennese Jews took pride in the fact that as a group they were better educated, were less involved in violent crimes, and had fewer children out of wedlock than the rest of Viennese society. Moreover, their general orientation was much more bourgeois than the overall population of Vienna, a fact that was deeply resented by Christians who were not. And, finally, Jewish writers and artists were very critical of many aspects of Viennese life. Overall, Jews were far from "humble," refusing to quietly fit into Viennese society. Even though their ancestors had been in Austria longer than those of many of their neighbors, Jews were considered outsiders, intruders, or foreigners who didn't quite belong.

In light of their poor public image and the gains that accrued to Viennese Christians, wholesale discrimination against Viennese Jews was indeed "sensible." Excluding Jews from professorships, bureaucratic positions, and student organizations meant more jobs and customers for non-Jews. Similarly, economic boycotts of Jewish companies meant more jobs and customers for non-Jews. Jews comprised almost half of Vienna's physicians and more than half of its lawyers. Excluding Jews from these professions, in a very tight and competitive job market, resulted in a major occupational advantage for Vienna's Christian population.

The vulnerability of German and Austrian Jews as a middleman minority, although arguably implicated in the development of genocidal policies on the part of the Nazi regime, is otherwise hardly unique. Hatred of middleman minorities underscores the competitive basis for much of prejudice. Throughout history, there have been certain groups of outsiders who have occupied an intermediate position between the economic elite and the masses of a particular society, often incurring the wrath of both groups. These middleman minorities often come from mother countries where they were well educated and middle class. In their host society, they typically come to play the role of small businesspeople and professionals. During periods of economic or political turmoil, middleman minorities have often been looted, vandalized, injured, murdered, and expelled. They have included Jews in Europe, Indians in East Africa, Chinese in the Philippines and Thailand, Cubans in Puerto Rico, and Koreans in the United States.

Middleman Minorities in the United States

Because of their position in the social structure, middleman minorities are frequently victimized not only by members of the dominant group but also by those underrepresented groups against whom they are forced to compete for small amounts of power, prestige, and wealth. Violent reaction to the middleman role of Korean Americans occurred in 1992 in the aftermath of the Rodney King beating and the subsequent trial and acquittal of the police officers involved in the attack. At the time of the Rodney King incident, many of the merchants in Black and Latino Los Angeles neighborhoods were of Korean descent. During the 1960s, many shopkeepers in Black neighborhoods were Jewish. Thus, Blacks saw Jews and then Koreans as outsiders who were taking advantage of them, didn't appreciate their business, were rude and arrogant, and had climbed the ladder of success over Black bodies to own shops and stores in the local neighborhood.

Of course, at least some part of the conflict, but not all of it, between Blacks and other groups may have been a result of cultural differences that could not be resolved. In fact, it is even reasonable to have predicted that Blacks might get along better with Jews or Koreans than with other Americans because these merchants down the block took a chance by opening marginally profitable businesses in places that were largely ignored by large corporations that opt for the vastly more profitable White suburbs or downtown shopping centers. As a result, stores in Black areas tend to be small, family-owned and -run businesses whose proprietors are required to work long hours to survive.

It is certainly not difficult to understand that in 1990s Los Angeles, at a time when they were feeling very much squeezed not only by Whites but by an increasing number of newcomers, Blacks would feel in competition with neighborhood merchants of Asian descent. Where groups differ in socially significant ways, for example, by race, religion, sexual orientation, disability status, or gender, there exists the potential for intergroup conflict. The potential is realized when the characteristics, attributes, or possessions of one group threaten (or are perceived to threaten) the well-being of another group. But the presence of a threatening difference doesn't necessarily lead to violence and discrimination, not unless there is also a sufficient degree of prejudice and hate to justify a collective effort to enslave, exile, or eliminate members of the threatening group. Thus, hate in the culture and personality provides the basis for doing harm to others by justifying an attack. When groups are in competition for scarce resources, their members are unlikely to get along. When hate and prejudice are available to characterize the opposing groups, animosity can easily turn into violence.

The American Version of Spectatorship

The forces of spectatorship at work so dramatically when Hitler's regime was in power have existed in countries around the world, including the United States. In the agrarian south, for example, slavery was widely viewed as a necessary aspect of the southern economic order generally and the plantation system of agricultural production in particular. But the one in four White southerners who owned slaves were not the only southerners who benefitted from the enslavement of Black Americans. Many more were spectators who never made money directly from slavery, but they did gain indirectly from the fact that Blacks were not allowed to compete with them for jobs and they enjoyed being members of what was considered a superior caste.

Moreover, the willingness of so many Americans during World War II to play the role of spectator made possible the rounding up of thousands of Japanese Americans, forcibly removing them from their homes, confiscating their property, and relocating them to interment camps (army-style barracks ringed with barbed wire and military guards) located thousands of miles away from their homes, where many of them remained throughout the war. Even before they were relocated in 1942, Japanese Americans had already been forced to give up their jobs and were subjected to a 6 a.m. to 6 p.m. curfew as well as a five-mile limit as to where they could travel from their homes (Kochiyama, 2001).

German and Italian Americans also suffered, but not so extensively, from the same policies to reduce domestic sources of sabotage. In fact, within 72 hours of the attack on Pearl Harbor, the FBI had almost 4000 Japanese, German, and Italian immigrants in custody. The government labeled hundreds of thousands of Italian immigrants as enemy aliens, forbidding them to leave their homes after dark, seizing their personal property, and forcing them to carry identification cards. Thousands of Italian immigrants were arrested and hundreds more were interned in military camps. Similarly, thousands of German immigrants were arrested and interned for the duration of the war. Unlike such policies regarding German Americans and Italian Americans, however, the government's treatment of Japanese Americans failed to distinguish native-born citizens from foreign-born newcomers. More than two-thirds of all Japanese Americans forced into internment camps were not immigrants. They were American citizens who were regarded as a security risk based only on their Japanese ancestry (Hummel, 1987; Holian, 1998). Using Executive Order 9066 as a legal basis, the federal government gave as its rationale that the United States was at war with Japan and simply could not afford to permit disloyal Americans of Japanese descent to sabotage the war effort. Not immigrant status, but racial identity (defined by identifying one Japanese great-grandparent) was the sole basis for being treated as the enemy and removed from American society.

Yet active cultural bigotry was only part of the story of sending Japanese Americans to interment camps. Knowing that they would be gone for some period of time, many of them sold their houses and personal property in a few days for next to nothing. Moreover, real estate agents eagerly bought up the land left by farmers of Japanese descent. Whites could have offered to rent the residences of their Japanese American neighbors and associates, but very few made the effort. Even though many White Americans recognized the unfairness of forcibly relocating an entire group of Americans, it was hard to discover anyone who had the courage—at the risk of being regarded as disloyal to the United States—to speak out against government policy (Kochiyama, 2001).

Even today in the arena of prejudice and hate, the largest number of Americans can probably be characterized as spectators. They appear to be indifferent or apathetic rather than hateful because they do little if anything to put an end to bigotry. Whatever their mind-set, their advocacy of values embodying the "American Creed"—democracy, equality of opportunity, and respect for diversity—is limited to verbalized agreement. As a matter of abstract principle, spectators may espouse support for the equal treatment of Blacks, Latinos, Asians, and White ethnics in the major public areas of everyday life—in schools, neighborhoods, workplaces, and public accommodations. In the context of everyday decision-making, however, they stand idly by, hoping not to get themselves involved, to look different, to stand apart from others, or perhaps they are even betting on being rewarded for their indifference.

In a recent questionnaire study, I discovered many college students who were spectators in the expression of hate and prejudice. In response to a racial slur or joke, they might feel offended, but they remain absolutely silent. One such student said:

> A co-worker was talking about the American Music Awards and how disgusting many of the "colored" people dressed and acted. I was so shocked that I didn't say anything—I just ignored it.

Another student reacted as follows to hearing the word "gay" repeatedly uttered by her friends to characterize others in a negative light:

> The word gets thrown around so often among a group of friends. It is used to insult each other. I guess I am fairly used to them saying it to each other, so that I don't even respond anymore. Yet, I would never say it.

Even if they believe in principles of democracy and equality of opportunity, spectators enjoy the advantages of bigotry. Rather than participate actively, they just go along to get along. They are bystanders to a situation that they may feel powerless to change. Of course, their very inactivity, their failure to act on their convictions, tends to give license to those who are raving bigots. At the same time, spectators benefit from whatever advantages their group receives from the perpetuation of prejudice. As a result, they laugh along with their friends at the most bigoted jokes, they walk right by teenagers painting hateful graffiti, and they make no effort to stop schemes aimed at harassing their Black neighbors.

CONCLUSION

Relatively few hate crimes are reported to the police every year, and most of those that are reported are committed not by members of organized hate groups but by dabblers in hate. In the typical hate offense, a group of bored and idle teenagers or young adults goes out on a Saturday night looking for someone to intimidate or assault. What often gets overlooked is that those who commit hate offenses are encouraged and supported by two categories of citizens: first, by sympathizers with bigotry who would perhaps never commit a hate offense themselves but are only too thrilled that others do. Those in sympathy with hate draw their thinking from the mainstream culture in which hate is widely learned and shared by members of a society. The second set of individuals probably represents the majority of citizens. Although they have not internalized the cultural stereotypes and emotions, they nevertheless remain passive bystanders in the face of destructive bigotry. These are the citizens who benefit from the status quo.

As we have seen, cultural standards alone cannot always explain the tremendous appeal of hate. Wherever prejudice becomes part of the culture of a society, where it is learned from an early age and widely shared, we can expect strong pressures for it to persist from generation to generation and to influence the behavior of society's members. At the same time, bigoted behavior persists not only because it becomes incorporated into cultural norms and roles and—at the individual level—is incorporated into the personality of hatemongers, dabblers, and sympathizers, but also because some of society's members believe they have a personal stake in their acceptance of hate and prejudice. We have seen, for example, how the leaders of various White supremacist groups are able to satisfy their craving to be important, while their followers gain a sense of belonging that was previously missing from their young lives (Ezekiel, 1995).

Sympathizers and spectators together create the conditions for hate crimes and ethnic violence to persist. To the extent that the culture of a society contains biased images of a particular group, then hate and prejudice will persist. For hate to be translated into hate crimes and intergroup violence, citizens must also believe that they are likely to benefit from bigotry and to suffer from tolerance. Those who are sympathetic to bigotry but who see no profit in supporting it will tend to express their hate verbally.

Indeed, even those individuals totally lacking in personal hatred may be supportive of bigoted behavior as a rational choice because they are convinced that a particular decision, even if distasteful in some of its aspects, will help to bring them the wealth, prestige, or power they believe that they so much deserve to possess or might keep them out of harm's way. It typically takes more than a sympathetic attitude toward hate to create the conditions conducive for hate crimes and discrimination to thrive and prosper; it also takes convincing a sufficient number of society's members that they will benefit from their decision in support of bigotry. In many cases, this means that they support the status quo, that they simply go along with the masses, and that they become not activists but passive spectators. Moreover, when hate is being considered as a viable political option, they might take an active stance in favor of a particular law, leader, political party, or public policy that supports or encourages hate. Under different circumstances, they might be respectful of differences; but when hate and prejudice are rewarded, they are seen to be what Merton (1957) referred to as "fair-weather" liberals.

Of course, such choices may not always perfectly reflect actual self-interest, only a perception that self-interest will benefit. The appeal of rational choice is complex, involving short- versus long-term interests; personal versus social identity; an array of objectives in the economic, psychological, and social spheres; and differences in access to information about a law, leader, political party, or policy (Brustein, 1996). The consequences of spectatorship may often be ambiguous, but the intentions are clear enough.

■ ■ ■ ■ ■ ▬▬▬▬▬▬▬▬▬▬▬▬▬▬▬▬▬▬▬▬▬▬

CHAPTER 3

THE BENEFITS OF BIGOTRY

PROTEST BY PROXY

To some extent, hate thrives on ignorance, and those who are poorly educated tend to be most prejudiced (Selznick and Steinberg, 1969; Chickering and Reisser, 1993). Yet, information or moral suasion alone does not always reduce bigotry. What may be more important, if less understood, is the fact that numerous Americans rich and poor, from all walks of life, actually *benefit* from being intolerant and hate-filled, or, at least they *believe* they benefit. Their gains may be short-term or long-term, imagined or real, economic, social, or psychological, but such individuals depend to a considerable extent on hate to give them a sense of well-being and adequacy, to reduce uncomfortable ambiguities in their everyday lives, and to sustain their socioeconomic advantages (Levin and Levin, 1982).

Culture certainly helps to assure that hate sticks around, that it is difficult to stop, and that it thrives and prospers across generations. Cultural prejudices help to identify the groups in society whose members are to be victimized and whose members are to be spared. At the same time, prejudice would never get started in the first place—wouldn't last 20 seconds—if it weren't for the fact that certain individuals and groups are benefitting from it.

The word "hate" in the term "hate crimes" can be misleading. As we have seen, those who commit thrill and mission hate crimes are frequently motivated by a desire to be accepted, to belong, to achieve a sense of importance and power, to gain attention, and to be in charge. Those who commit defensive hate offenses often possess an economic motivation; they seek to keep their jobs or to improve their property values. The cultural stereotypes specify which groups are appropriate to attack, but they do not, by themselves, provide the motivation. This can be seen in the lack of specialization among many hatemongers. If they can't find someone Black to assault, they will go after someone gay. If they can't find someone who is gay, they will victimize an individual who is Latino, or Jewish, or disabled, or Catholic (Levin and McDevitt, 2002).

Certain questions are very telling. Would, for example, there have been a holocaust in Nazi Germany if Jews had not existed? Given the power of what Daniel Goldhagen (1996) calls an "eliminationist Anti-Semitism" in German culture and history, you might conclude "probably not." At the same time, considering the horrible economic conditions in Germany during the 1930s and the humiliating post–World War I international policies that brought Germany to its knees, you might conclude that some groups would still have been targeted, even if not at a genocidal level of destruction. And we know that Hitler victimized not only Jews but also gays, the elderly, the disabled, gypsies, Poles, and the mentally ill.

Would there have been slavery in the United States in the absence of Africans to play the role of slaves? Probably yes. Hate helped to justify enslaving Blacks, but the impulse to find a source of cheap labor was totally independent of prejudice or racism. For a period of time, American Indians were enslaved. For a period of time, Whites of European descent became indentured servants who were treated as slaves for a finite period after which time they earned their freedom. If it hadn't been Africans who were enslaved, it might have been the members of some other "devalued" group.

During the 1960s, when hundreds of civil disturbances spread across the country, Black Americans in large urban centers like Los Angeles looted and destroyed most of the shops and stores in their neighborhoods, many of which were owned and operated by White Jews. Would these stores have been ransacked and burned if their proprietors had not been Jewish? The answer is probably yes. The evidence can be seen in the early 1990s when the Black and Latino residents of Los Angeles' inner-city neighborhoods destroyed thousands of stores and shops owned by Korean Americans.

Given their vulnerability, racial and religious minorities are frequently targets of displaced aggression for members of society who are profoundly frustrated in their efforts to be successful and, for one reason or another, cannot express their hostility toward the true source of their problems. Instead, they engage in *protest by proxy*. That is, they scapegoat on a collective level by constructing an evil force, an enemy, that becomes the perceived source of their predicament and the object of their animosity and therefore deserving punishment.

The deep recession of the early 1980s convinced some destitute and out-of-work automobile workers, farmers, ranchers, miners, and workers in the timber industry that Jews, Asians, and Blacks were responsible for all of their economic woes. Up to the late 1980s, during the so-called "cold war" era, many Americans traced their personal problems to the conspiratorial activities of the "evil empire" located in the vast and powerful republics under the control of the Soviet Union.

With the demise of eastern European communism, however, it became more difficult to externalize responsibility for America's miseries.

The enemy had to be reconstructed. Instead of locating evil in Moscow, more and more Americans found it in Washington, D.C.; New York; and Hollywood. Since the 1970s, the credibility of all leadership positions in the United States (government, science, medicine, education, business, and even religion) has seriously eroded. Fewer and fewer Americans now believe that people in positions of power represent the interests of the average citizen. In fact, some are convinced that communists have taken over the White House, the Supreme Court, and Congress (Halpern and Levin, 1996; Karl, 1995). In a recent Gallup poll, less than 20 percent of all Americans rated the honesty and ethics of the following occupational groups as "high" or "very high": lawyers, senators, labor union leaders, stockbrokers, congressmen, car salesmen, telemarketers, business executives, and advertising practitioners (Jones, 2005).

Protest by proxy gives a sense of satisfaction not possible if one attacks vague and abstract economic and social forces. Thus, instead of blaming global competition, corporate downsizing, and automation for putting them out of work, some Americans prefer to put a human (or subhuman) face on the enemy: communists in the White House, the Satanic Jewish lobby, Blacks and Latinos who unjustly receive special treatment and privileges, or the menace of immigration.

Protest by proxy is connected with a long history of violence being perpetrated, during periods of economic turmoil and bad times, against vulnerable and marginalized groups. Between 1800 and 1930, whenever the cotton crops failed in southern states, Blacks were lynched. At low points in the business cycle, Ku Klux Klan (KKK) membership rose. During the Great Depression of the 1930s, there were 114 organizations whose purpose was to spread anti-Semitism, and there were numerous nativist organizations whose purpose was to reduce the flow of immigrants to zero. It is hard to bash an abstraction; for someone whose life has been torn apart by failure, it may be much more psychologically satisfying to burn a house of worship, to blow up a building, or to bludgeon someone to death with a baseball bat.

As introduced in Chapter 2, protest by proxy has been expressed in what some observers have labeled the *new anti-Semitism* (Iganski and Kosmin, 2003; Chesler, 2003). Thoroughly outraged by American policies that support an Israeli presence in the Middle East and anti-immigrant policies in European countries, some Muslims and Arabs as well as Europeans have adopted a posture of hostility and conflict. But rather than aim their attack directly at the west, at capitalism, at the United States, or even at Israelis, certain extremists have instead attacked a more vulnerable group—Jews around the world.

In September 2005, a series of cartoons depicting the Islamic prophet Mohammed unfavorably (e.g., as a suicide bomber) were published in the Danish newspaper *Jyllands-Posten*. By February 1, 2006, the same satirical cartoons had appeared in newspapers across the world from

Switzerland to Australia, from Germany to Japan. In response, outraged Muslims hurled gasoline bombs and stones at Danish embassies. In the Middle East, Asia, and Africa, tens of thousands of angry Muslims demonstrated in the streets. Police opened fire on Afghan rioters as they attacked a base of Norwegian NATO troops with grenades and guns. After threats against their lives were issued, the cartoonists whose drawings had inspired a firestorm of protest in the Muslim world reportedly went into hiding under police protection.

The extremity of the Muslim response may, in part, be a function of differences in theology. For Muslims, depicting the prophet Mohammed in satirical form was nothing short of blasphemous. Westerners were viewed by millions of observant Muslims as initiating a vicious attack on Islamic religious beliefs. From the Muslim point of view, publishing cartoons degrading Mohammed was only the latest in a long series of insensitive acts committed against Islam by westerners. When asked in a Gallup survey what western countries could do to improve relations with the Muslim/Arab world, the most common reply from citizens of predominantly Islamic nations (from Morocco to Indonesia) was that they should demonstrate greater respect and tolerance for Islam (Esposito, 2006).

In addition, even prior to the September 11, 2001 attack on America, many White Europeans were already voicing, in angry and intolerant tones, their concern that an influx of guest workers and refugees was changing the basic character of their countries—and not for the better. Increasing numbers of Europeans began to support right-wing political movements aimed at reducing the flow of immigration. For example, a March 2000 Harris survey determined that 60 percent of French adults believed that too many people of "foreign origin" were in France; 63 percent told pollsters there were too many Arabs (Australia Immigration Visa Services, 2000).

After September 11, 2001, the conflict only worsened. Muslims were very much aware of the heightened wave of anti-Muslim sentiment sweeping through European nations, part of which was but one aspect of an increasing intolerance for any group regarded as "foreign." A 2005 Harris poll of adults in Great Britain found 73 percent agreeing that "the current government has been too lax with regards to its immigration policy" (Harris Interactive, 2005). A recent survey of violent hate crimes concluded that since the 9-11 attack on America, a message of xenophobia has infiltrated political movements throughout Europe (McClintock, 2005).

In Denmark, where the cartoons satirizing Mohammed were originally published, an anti-immigrant party won 12 percent of the vote in a parliamentary election in November 2001. Opinion surveys reported that a growing number of Danish citizens were resentful of foreigners, seeing them as welfare recipients, terrorists, and criminals. Campaign posters portraying a young blonde girl said: "When she retires, Denmark will have a Muslim majority" (Finn, 2002, A1).

It would seem all but inconceivable for Islamic leaders rationally to blame Jews for producing blasphemous images of Mohammad, but that didn't stop them from going on an anti-Jewish tirade. Rather than attack Christianity, for example, one of Iran's most popular newspapers announced sponsorship of a contest to locate the best Holocaust cartoon (Birsel, 2006). This response was seen as particularly vengeful, in light of the recent statements attributed to Iran's president Mahmoud Ahmadine-jad that the holocaust carried out by the Nazis was a myth (Australian Broadcasting Corporation, 2005). More recently, Iran's supreme religious leader Ayatollah Ali Khamenei called the offensive cartoons a "Zionist conspiracy" (Associated Press, 2005).

Ironically, Arab Americans and Muslim Americans have also become victims of protest by proxy. Americans eager to place the responsibility for the September 11 terrorist attack found it less than psychologically satisfying to blame some shadowy figure named Osama bin Laden, located thousands of miles away, whom they had seen a few times over the years on low-quality videotapes or in fuzzy newspaper photographs. In sharp contrast, their Muslim American and Arab American neighbors and coworkers were easier to identify and close at hand. Some wore headscarves and veils; many stopped to pray several times daily. They had foreign-sounding accents and dark skin. They weren't the terrorists aboard the doomed airplanes that hit the Pentagon and World Trade Center, but they shared enough characteristics with these Middle-Eastern terrorists to provide a convenient scapegoat (Levin and Rabrenovic, 2004b).

PSYCHOLOGICAL ADVANTAGES

In the short run, hate generates some important psychological advantages. It gives a temporary boost to self-esteem and makes sense of a world that might otherwise seem chaotic and unpredictable. Rather than do the hard work of dealing directly with their problems, bigots continue to cover them up, sidestep them, deny that they exist. In the long run, hate has the capacity to destroy those who hate or, at the very least, make their lives miserable. But in the meantime, they receive a much needed boost to their egos and the basis for living in an apparently predictable world.

Enhancing and Protecting Self-Esteem

Hate directed against a specific group of people is learned. It is not inborn. Individuals learn to be bigots; they are taught which groups to despise, which groups to avoid, and which groups to oppose. At the same time, there may be predispositions, developed through evolution and programmed at birth into the human being, that tend universally to foster a preference for an individual's own group members and that might contribute to hate if not effectively controlled (Fishbein, 1996).

Individuals tend to identify with groups. Their self-esteem may be some function of how they feel about themselves and how they feel about their group memberships. Thus, they may experience higher self-esteem if they think their group is superior; they may feel worse about themselves if they consider their group inferior to others. Social identity affects personal identity (Brown, 1986; Fishbein, 1996).

According to research by Tajfel et al. (1971), it is merely the act of being assigned to a group (any minimal group) that creates the full in-group preference. In other words, just being assigned by the flip of a coin to a group named A rather than to a group called B is enough to make an individual prefer group A over group B. Therefore, just because of their membership in the group, many people tend to attribute positive characteristics and good deeds to individuals in the group to which they belong and negative characteristics and bad deeds to everybody else (Billig and Tajfel, 1973; Locksley et al., 1980). Strangers may be devalued simply because they are outsiders who don't belong (Beck, 1999). Moreover, there is a tendency for individuals to better remember the good behavior of the in-group and to better remember the bad behavior of the out-group (Rothbard, Evans, and Fulero, 1979).

The phenomenon of "minimal group favoritism" seems to exist, but it hardly explains the levels of violence, hate, and destruction (genocide, slavery, mass murder) that have been aimed throughout history at the members of various out-groups. Nor does the minimal group effect explain wide variations in the groups selected for victimization—Muslims in one circumstance, Jews in another, Latinos in still another, and so on.

Social psychologists have long argued for the existence of a personality type that encourages the scapegoating of vulnerable victims. Prejudice is part of our culture, but it also serves an important psychological need for self-esteem and respectability. The target of prejudice is selected because he has been widely stereotyped as inferior, as dirty or lazy or stupid or immoral or alcoholic or sly or treacherous or whatever. Through a process of social comparison, the perpetrator is able to gain a sense of her own superiority, for example, as beautiful, smart, or moral, only to the extent that she places the victim in an inferior position.

This zero-sum definition of respectability can be found in early versions of a work called *The Authoritarian Personality* (Adorno et al., 1950). It describes a psychoanalytic theory generated by a group of refugees from Nazi Germany who sought to locate in early childhood the genesis of anti-Semitism and other forms of bigotry. According to the original conception, the authoritarian personality was a syndrome of symptoms in which prejudice was the basic pathology. First, from this point of view, authoritarians are *ethnocentric,* that is, they express a generalized hostility toward a range of groups considered by cultural norms to be weak or inferior. If they hate Blacks, ethnocentrics are likely to despise Jews, Latinos, and Asians as well. Characteristics of the victim are more or less irrelevant and take a backseat psychologically to the authoritarian aggressor's need for power, dominance, and control. To overcome their feelings of inferiority and powerlessness, authoritarians come to identify with powerful figures (e.g., with Hitler) and to despise any and all groups stereotyped as weak or inferior. Second, authoritarians tend to have extreme right-wing political views. They are antidemocratic; they are fascists and ardent anticommunists who resemble Hitler and his henchmen in terms of political ideology. Third, according to this theory, prejudice has its roots in harsh and threatening child-rearing practices. Imitation of a youngster's parents' bigoted attitudes is not regarded as an important source of hate; instead, it is the way in which the child is raised that determines whether he eventually develops a psychological need for prejudice and takes an authoritarian perspective. Thus, the young child in an authoritarian family is rigidly relegated to the role of the dependent and submissive underling. The child is subjected to severe, even brutal, discipline. Because of being maltreated at an early age, the bigoted youngster grows up feeling a profound sense of powerlessness. As an adult, to compensate, he identifies with powerful elements of society and seeks to distance himself from groups stereotyped as inferior, weak, and powerless (Adorno et al., 1950). This is the basis for his hate.

In literally thousands of studies since the 1950s, many of the ideas contained in the theory of the authoritarian personality have been confirmed and others have been rejected or qualified. In the original view, for example, prejudice was associated exclusively with an extreme right-wing political orientation. In light of the systematic anti-Semitism of Hitler's fascist regime from which they had escaped, it seemed to the creators of the theory that fascism and bigotry were integrally connected. They could not imagine what subsequent research would reveal, namely, that prejudice can be located at any point along the political spectrum. Thus, there are bigots on the left, bigots on the right, and bigots in the middle. Indeed, there are even some bigots who are entirely without any political position at all (Rokeach, 1952).

More recently, social psychologists have turned their attention to what they call a social dominance orientation, a term that identifies individuals who want their own group to predominate and be superior to other groups (Sidanius, Pratto, and Bobo, 1994). Those who have a social dominance orientation agree with the following statements: "Some people are just more worthy than others." "It is sometimes necessary to step on others to get ahead in life." "Some groups are simply not the equal of others." Individuals oriented to social dominance believe that superior groups (including their own, of course) are deserving of greater wealth and power and that inferior groups are deserving of far less. In an effort to justify such beliefs, those with a social dominance perspective often accept the negative stereotypes and prejudices in their culture that characterize minority groups in a negative light (Pratto et al., 1994). Such sub-human images make it possible to behave with moral impunity in accordance with social dominance beliefs.

It is interesting to note the important role of bigotry in various efforts and movements apparently designed to enhance the sense of power and dominance of individuals who have so little of either. The two young members of the "Trenchcoat Mafia" who in April 1999 went on a shooting spree at their Littleton, Colorado, high school timed their attack to occur on Hitler's birthday. Just as they had planned, the two young shooters, Harris and Klebold, even in death gained the attention of the nation. This is apparently precisely what they craved. They wanted to be important by having a major, if deadly, impact on those who had rejected them: classmates, teachers, and society at large. Similarly, Dion Terres, a young man who killed two people randomly in a Kenosha, Wisconsin, McDonald's and then took his own life, was hardly a dedicated Nazi; yet he had hung a large Nazi flag in his living room as a symbol of power and dominance. Terres felt that he had lost all control over his life and blamed his family and friends for all of his misfortunes. Just before going on a rampage, he expressed his admiration for Hitler's quest for world domination, an effort that came very close to succeeding.

I hate to admit it, but I have appeared several times on the Jerry Springer show. In my own defense, I hasten to add that I was on Springer when he was actually an intellectual and moral notch above most of the other talk show hosts. Shortly after my last appearance, his ratings plummeted (could my appearance have helped?) and so apparently did his ethical standards.

On my final visit, I was on Springer along with three racist skin-heads[1] who appeared dressed in Nazi uniforms complete with armbands. One also had a Charles Manson–like swastika tattoo etched in the middle of his forehead. It became very clear over the course of the program that these three young men were totally unsophisticated with respect to Nazi or White supremacist ideology or history. It occurred to me then that the three skinheads could just as easily have joined a gang or a cult. They were marginalized youngsters who weren't getting along at home,

---

[1]It should be noted that not all skinheads are racists. In fact, there are groups of antiracist skinheads, gay skinheads, and people of color who are in skinhead groups. The common denominator among all such skinhead groups seems to be a willingness to use violence as a means for resolving differences.

weren't making it at school with their peers, and had little hope of ever having anything more than dead-end jobs. But they were looking desperately to feel important. The Nazi uniforms and tattoo had only one purpose for them: to give them a sense of power. At home and at school, they were treated like outcastes. But among their Nazi skinhead friends, they felt special, in charge of things, like big shots.[2]

Many hatemongers who join racist skinhead groups gain a great deal on the psychological level (Ezekiel, 1995; Hamm, 1994). Growing up, many of them were never entirely accepted by their peers. Instead, other students considered them geeks, nerds, weirdos, or bullies. Many were like Harris and Klebold, the mass murderers at Columbine High School. And not unlike Harris and Klebold, many hatemongers rely heavily on fellow outcasts for their sense of identity, belonging, and importance.

Since the April 1999 massacre of students at Columbine High School, the issue of bullying has become newsworthy. The two youthful shooters decided to get even after reportedly being harassed, intimidated, and rejected by their schoolmates. For 13 months, they planned their suicidal attack and collected an arsenal of weapons, including semi-automatic firearms and explosives with which they intended to slay hundreds of their schoolmates and teachers and to blow up the school building. In the end, they killed 13 and inspired numerous alienated students around the country to seek revenge by pulling false alarms, threatening to do physical harm, or opening fire in their classrooms.

After the massacre at Columbine High, it was reported that Klebold and Harris had idolized Hitler and hated Jews and people of color. They also despised the athletes in their school who enjoyed the popularity and admiration of their peers. Not coincidentally, Klebold and Harris's first victim was a Black student athlete.

Unfortunately, the recent attention given to bullying in public schools arose out of a collective desire to identify students who might get angry enough to murder their classmates. Although understandable, this motivation fails to recognize two important things about bullying: first, it is a pervasive problem, having profoundly impacted the lives of countless

---

[2]Because this may not seem very important, I am placing it in a footnote. When I appeared on Springer, during a commercial break, the producer instructed me to be seated next to one of the three skinheads on the program. Not realizing that his mike was open and that he could be overheard in the control room, the skinhead pointed in my direction and whispered to one of his buddies, "I feel like killing this guy." At this point, the producer rushed onto the set and informed me of the conversation between the skinhead guests. Of course, I did the prudent thing and asked that she move me to a position on the stage where it would be harder to get me. One more thing is worth reporting. After the show, while being driven to the airport, the three skinheads asked the driver to stop the car and let them out in downtown Chicago. Still wearing their Nazi uniforms, they immediately walked into a Burger King and only came out when the police arrived and carted them off to jail. I understand they were charged with assault.

students around the country who, because of some difference from the norm, simply do not measure up to the expectations of their peers; second, that bullying is a longstanding problem, having afflicted students not just during the past few years but for many decades.

Very few bullied students get even with their tormentors, but they continue to harbor resentment and hate not only for their classmates but also for any group considered weak by conventional standards. Many more internalize the stigma and grow up believing that they are inferior. Others become social isolates who come to have a general distrust of other people. Some who experience an intimidating school environment claim that their lives are destroyed; most are at least uncomfortable during their years of attending middle and high school (Bonds and Stoker, 2000). Still others become the authoritarian personalities addressed in the theory of authoritarianism and eventually identify with the aggressor. They become the biggest bullies on the block and victimize any student who shows weakness or frailty.

Being from a different race, religion, nationality, or sexual orientation is frequently a basis for victimization by bullies. In March 2001, a 14-year-old girl in Wiliamsport, Pennsylvania, allegedly shot her classmate in the shoulder with her father's .22 caliber handgun. Reportedly, the suspect was protecting an Asian student who had been bullied and harassed by the shooting victim (Reuters, 2001).

Gay students, or those students who appear to be gay, seem to be victimized with special enthusiasm. They get used to finding the word "fag" spelled out in pink lipstick on their lockers or having to confront the taunting words "faggot" or "dyke" just inches from the face of their tormentor (Berrill, 1992). The bullying occasionally takes an especially ugly turn. In one suburban Omaha high school, for example, a senior recently found a note in his mailbox written in boldface in purple letters, "All fags must die. You first" (Laue, 2000).

In a recent case of harassment involving a physical disability, a student in Stanwood, Washington, recounted her many years of enduring the intimidating and taunting behavior of her schoolmates. The 19-year-old woman, Taya Haugstad, who was born with cerebral palsy in Calcutta, India, was, from the fifth grade on, the target of intimidation by other students who mocked her body movements, taunted her with obscenities and name-calling, and blocked her wheelchair. In middle school, another student forced Haugstad's hand from the joystick that controlled her wheelchair, causing Haugstad to swerve into a wall and strike her head (DeMillo, 2000; Stevick, 2000).

In response to the constant bullying, Haugstad often put her head in her hands and cried. She begged her tormentors to stop. At night, she cried in her sleep and experienced nightmares in which she relived the harassing behavior she had received during the school day. By the time she reached high school, the young woman had completely withdrawn.

Reducing Uncertainty

In addition to enhancing or protecting self-esteem, hate also provides individuals with the schema or cognitive blueprint they seek in order to organize, recall, and make sense out of the ambiguities of everyday experiences. Stereotyping gives hatemongers an important edge by making their world seem predictable. *Blacks are lazy; Whites can't be trusted; Latinos are dirty; Asians are rude; Women are emotional; Irish are pugnacious; Jews are mercenary; Muslims are terrorists;* and so on. Such information comes not from the difficult process of getting to know someone; it is simply assumed to be true based on preconceived images (Wyer and Srull, 1994).

Prejudiced individuals tend to be intolerant of ambiguities. They desire absolute and unequivocal feelings about themselves and others and emphasize and exaggerate strengths in themselves and the accomplishments of their own group. They focus only on the weaknesses of out-group members (Steiner and Johnson, 1963; Triandis and Triandis, 1972).

Locating the enemy takes on particular importance for a hatemonger. In an early study, Rokeach (1952) found that extremely prejudiced subjects were afraid to admit defeat when confronted with the challenging task of correctly matching names with the faces of strangers. Whereas prejudiced subjects made numerous erroneous guesses, subjects with less prejudice more often admitted being confused and were less willing to take wild guesses.

In 1972, Quanty, Keats, and Harkins found that anti-Semites were more willing to label a face Jewish on the basis of limited information than were tolerant individuals. When asked to identify a number of photographs as Jewish or non-Jewish, the anti-Semites thought that they saw more Jews but were also more inaccurate than their unprejudiced counterparts. "They seem more concerned with correctly identifying Jews than they are with falsely labeling a person Jewish" (Quanty, Keats, and Harkins, 1975, p. 454).

The results obtained in a more recent study suggest that very prejudiced people give an inordinate amount of attention to information about the group of people they hate. When asked to determine the racial identity of a racially ambiguous stranger, they take significantly more time to make a decision (Blascovich et al., 1997). Moreover, prejudiced individuals remember with greater accuracy the information that supports their stereotypical beliefs than the information that contradicts them (Fiske and Neuberg, 1990).

ECONOMIC AND STATUS ADVANTAGES

As we have seen, some historians have suggested that the appeal of Nazism took advantage of widespread sympathy for a unique theme of hate in mainstream German culture. In this view, Hitler came to power because of his eliminationist anti-Semitism in which Jews were portrayed as the vermin responsible for all of Germany's economic woes. According to Brustein (1996), however, rational choice rather than bigotry may have been responsible for much of the success of the Nazi party in its early efforts to garner popular support and increase its membership rolls. Those who voted for and actively supported the Nazi movement were German citizens who believed they had the most to gain from its success.

Self-interest, or at least the perception of self-interest, may be at the basis of much intergroup hostility. In the expression of hate, perpetrators, sympathizers, and spectators all stand to benefit in a very material sense. Bigotry provides the members of society and its rulers with a number of important economic and status advantages.

Getting the Dirty Work Done

In every society, certain jobs and responsibilities are seen as sinful, undignified, menial, or physically dirty. They may also be regarded as absolutely essential for the well-being of the population or its rulers. Throughout history, much of a society's dirtiest work has been reserved for those individuals relegated to a position outside the mainstream, frequently those who are already stigmatized and vulnerable.

The history of the Jews is replete with such examples. During the Middle Ages, whenever they were regarded by those in power as capable of playing a valuable role, Jews were tolerated and frequently treated respectfully. Beginning in the sixth century, Jews were invited to settle in France, Germany, and Italy so that they could help develop city life, spread trade and commerce, and serve in the monarch's court as advisors and diplomats. The feudal system of the day consisted of nobles, priests, and serfs; it did not include a merchant class. Thus, Jews were left with an important role to play. They soon became Europe's middle class—its merchants, bankers, artisans, judges, and jewelers.

In their position outside both the feudal system and Catholicism, Jews were uniquely qualified to perform the essential service of lending money at interest, an activity absolutely forbidden on religious grounds to the Christian majority. The medieval church considered the lending of money sinful regardless of the amount of interest charged or the purpose for which money was borrowed. Thus, a Christian who today receives 3 percent interest on a savings account would, during the Middle Ages, have committed a mortal sin. Yet, money lending was, at the same time, considered necessary by both the church and the nobility as a source of outside financing for building, farming, waging war, and engaging in political affairs. In the eyes of the medieval church, Jews were already headed for damnation; their participation in money-lending could add little to the eternal punishment that awaited them in the hereafter. Thus, Christians used Jews to perform important banking functions they could not perform themselves in the same way that Jews often used their Christian neighbors to conduct affairs on the Sabbath that they themselves were prohibited by religious tradition from conducting (Dimont, 1962).

Similarly, the presence of dirty yet essential tasks motivated the development of slavery in the New World. The enslavement of Blacks may have derived its initial impetus from an acute labor shortage existing in colonial America that could not be resolved satisfactorily by means of European manpower. At least half of the White European immigrants to colonial America paid their passage to the New World by obligating themselves as servants for periods of from two to seven years (Stampp, 1956). When sources of White labor threatened to dry up, America shifted its attention to Africa.

Southerners could have turned entirely to White labor, but they would have sacrificed the several advantages that only slavery could have provided. First, an average White laborer was paid more than the cost of investing in and maintaining his enslaved counterpart. Second, the slave owner was far better able to exploit Black women and children. Third, a master could require his slaves to work longer hours under more difficult conditions without having to negotiate with his workers or with their labor unions. Finally, slave ownership was a symbol of status that identified the master with a privileged social class in the South (Stampp, 1956). As we have seen, the absolute distinction between free and slave labor that developed on the basis of race alone assured that all Whites could feel they were members of a superior racial group. Moreover, slavery was a method for limiting competition from Blacks (Wilhelm, 1970).

Less obviously, the many White northerners who benefited from slavery in the South contributed to its development and maintenance. Many of the ships that carried slaves to plantations in the South were owned by northern merchants and built in northern shipyards. The slave trade in the northern colonies spawned numerous ancillary businesses such as cotton mills, rum distilleries, and iron foundries. Northern insurance companies benefited by insuring slaves, and northern newspapers ran advertisements in which they urged citizens to return runaway slaves in return for large cash rewards. Northern blacksmiths made the chains to keep slaves from escaping and manufactured the barrels for rum whiskey (Robertson and Kerber, 2000).

For a period of time, American Indians also were enslaved by the White colonials, but several factors mitigated against making American Indians into slaves as a general policy. First, their adaptation to plantation life was impeded by cultural factors. Second, American Indians could often escape to the protection of their own tribes that lived near the plantation. Third, early White settlers feared neighboring tribes and sought their friendship more than their labor. As a result, a predominantly African ancestry became the requirement for enslavement (Stampp, 1956).

In the southern colonies, a few powerful Americans, predominantly planters, shared a need for numerous slaves who could be trained and controlled for profitable exploitation (Noel, 1968). As a result, the vast majority of southern slaves filled the roles of field hands and domestic servants, and a smaller number of slaves were employed as needed in saltworks, mines, railroad construction, textile mills, and in other occupations that required specialized skills (Logan, 1954). Also as a result of the need for exploitable labor, slavery soon came to be regarded as a kind of "White man's burden," as a moral and religious obligation on the part of White southerners that was divinely ordained and ultimately beneficial to the "uncivilized" and "inferior" Black slave (Comer, 1972; Genovese, 1969; Levin and Levin, 1982).

The changing character of California's farm workers over many decades illustrates the influence of sheer availability on the fate of those selected to do low-paying and physically challenging jobs. American Indians were California's first farm workers, arriving on the scene at a time when agricultural production was restricted to cattle and wheat. But a subsequent influx of Chinese immigrants soon changed the nature of farm work in California. By 1870, as work on the transcontinental railroad was coming to an end, Chinese laborers turned for work to California's farmland. Partly because of the availability of a large supply of Chinese workers, the state's agricultural patterns shifted from livestock and wheat to fruits and vegetables, crops requiring much larger amounts of hand labor.

The supply of abundant Chinese labor continued until 1882, when Congress suspended Chinese immigration. At about the same time, however, the Japanese government lifted its ban on emigration, permitting sizable numbers of workers from the rice paddies of Japan to travel to the west coast of the United States. Until the early decades of the twentieth century, when anti-Japanese sentiment arose in full force, Japanese immigrants were a major source of farm labor in California. After 1910, however, the upheaval of revolution south of the border persuaded tens of thousands of rural Mexicans to flee to the safety of the United States. From that time to the present day, Mexicans have continued to represent the most important source of California's farm labor.

Eliminating Opponents

Getting the dirty work done is hardly the only economic benefit derived from hate and prejudice. Depending on prevailing economic circumstances, the members of a society may become more active in seeking new avenues for assuring their own economic and status survival. When they are threatened, some may attempt to eliminate their competitors for scarce resources. Because of their vulnerability as stigmatized "outsiders," minority group members make especially effective targets of hate and hostility.

Until the eleventh century, the medieval church was, in large part, tolerant of its Jewish citizens, including those who refused to convert to Christianity. In the early centuries of the Middle Ages, Catholics continued to cling to the hope that Jews would someday see the light and abandon their mistaken religious beliefs in favor of the superior Christian alternative. In most quarters, violence was simply not regarded as a necessary proselytizing tactic. Instead, Jews were excluded from the feudal system so that their heretical beliefs and rituals could not contaminate the Christian majority. Still, the Jewish role was considered an important one.

But large-scale persecution of European Jewry began in earnest during the eleventh century as the opening campaigns of the Crusades swept the land, and not only Jews but Muslims as well as recalcitrant non-Christians became potential victims of brutality. Those who refused to convert were seen as a threat to the veracity of the Christian version of a universal deity. Jews were banished from several European countries or fled to escape being massacred.

Motivations for the Crusades were mixed. Countless numbers of Crusaders were devout Christians who sincerely sought to spread the word of God to the infidel. Others had an ulterior and more worldly motive, however: for their participation, sinners were absolved, criminals were pardoned, and serfs were granted their freedom. Still others joined the Crusades to plunder the wealthy or simply to delight in killing with impunity.

Charges of diabolical Jewish religious rituals suddenly were heard repeated by those who were eager to justify their murderous onslaught. Many argued that Jews murdered Christian children to spray their blood over the Passover matzoh (unleavened bread) as part of an ancient holiday ritual. Or that Jews re-enacted the crucifixion by stealing the communion wafer (representing the body of Christ) and stabbing it with a sharp knife until it bled. Rumors spread that Jews possessed an odor of evil that miraculously disappeared upon their conversion to Christianity. According to other rumors, Jews were held responsible for poisoning the wells of Europe, thereby causing the epidemic of Black Death that swept through many European cities with devastating impact, frequently killing Christians and Jews alike (Weiss, 1996).

Such anti-Jewish stereotypes spread just as the policies of church and state began to shift profoundly in the direction of intolerance and discrimination. The dehumanization of European Jewry effectively supported not only religious persecution but economic disengagement as well. By the year 1200, recognizing the advantages of the money-lending role, Christians began to supplant Jewish bankers. As the feudal system disintegrated around them, Jews were forced out of their positions in the business community, generally to make room for Christians who sought to eliminate their Jewish competitors. By law, Jews were now forced to wear yellow badges on their clothing and were moved into ghettos. When economic conditions worsened and the masses threatened to revolt, Jews rather than ineffective fiscal policies were held responsible. Beginning with England, they found themselves banished from country after country.

The Black experience in the United States has been similarly affected by the extent to which political circumstances have set the stage for Blacks and Whites to compete. There were many slaveowners who argued that Whites had an obligation to maintain their system of enslaving Blacks to assure that they would survive. In the antebellum South, slaves who at least overtly went along with the system and were willing to "stay in their place" tended to be stereotyped as "little Black Sambo" types, as children who lacked the intelligence and initiative to make it as free people.

After the Civil War, however, the presence of Whites in direct competition with ex-slaves for jobs assured the perpetuation of the myth that Blacks were somehow innately ill-equipped for precisely the same skilled work they had competently performed before being emancipated (Bonacich, 1972; Harris, 1964). This was the case, even though an absolute level of segregation and humiliation of Blacks did not set in until the turn of the century, long after decades of racial conflict and competition led by a "relaxation of the opposition" to racism had established a firm hold on the character of American society (Woodward, 1955).

During the period following the end of the Civil War known as Reconstruction, at a time when they had a genuine possibility of gaining economic and political clout, Blacks found themselves stereotyped more as dangerous animals than as naive children. The new image justified not keeping Blacks dependent and submissive, as they had been expected to be during slavery, but treating Blacks as subhumans who, in self-defense, needed to be segregated, repressed, and even killed (Levin and Levin, 1982).

During Reconstruction, the enslavement of Blacks was replaced by increasing episodes of hate violence. From the standpoint of White southerners, the enemy between 1865 and 1877 consisted of reform-minded northerners who sought to "reconstruct" the vanquished South and Black leaders who hoped to divide large plantations into a number of small farms to give to former slaves. The Republican party sought to enlarge its influence by enlisting the allegiance of newly freed slaves, liberal southerners, and abolitionist northerners who had traveled to the southern states in an effort to achieve reform (Lane, 1997). Constituting what Roger Lane (1997) refers to as a guerrilla war of national liberation, new and more deadly tactics were needed to restore the power enjoyed by the dominant White majority before secession.

With the help of the Union army, the federal government remained in charge of many everyday affairs. It was, however, much too segmented, inconsistent, and uncommitted to see to it that White southerners would accept an increased role for Blacks in the power structure of the South. Instead, the southern majority turned to tactics of intimidation, assault, and murder to keep ex-slaves in only the dirtiest, lowest-paying jobs— those unacceptable to Whites—and to keep them from voting. By the year 1877, when the federal troops withdrew and relations between Blacks and Whites were returned to local White southerners, there had been countless incidents of lynchings, riots, and murders committed by individual southerners as well as secret societies including the Ku Klux Klan.

Fear of economic warfare from newly freed slaves became intense among working-class Whites who until the abolition of slavery had enjoyed state support in keeping Black Americans from competing for their jobs. One White worker, writing at the turn of the century, represented the thinking of many White southerners about the "race question":

> Take a young Negro of little more than ordinary intelligence, even, get hold of him in time, train him thoroughly as to books, and finish him up with a good industrial education, send him out into the South with ever so good intentions both on the part of his benefactor and himself, send him to take my work away from me and I will kill him. (Franklin and Starr, 1967, p. 25)

In the reinstatement of local White rule came a permanent system of institutionalized segregation and an onslaught of hate crimes directed against ex-slaves who were audacious enough to continue seeking a share of the power and wealth of White southerners. In Texas, Kentucky, and South Carolina, the murder rate was approximately 18 times that for the New England states. Throughout the South, White on Black murder rates skyrocketed to the point that they represented some 80 percent of all such homicides nationally. By the 1890s, lynchings of Blacks in southern states had peaked to about 100 yearly. Murder in the South had become social policy.

Although morally reprehensible, there is little doubt that murder was an extremely effective policy for reinstating the rule of Whites and the subjugation of Blacks. During Reconstruction, millions of Blacks for the first time voted and millions more competed for the first time in the job market against White opponents. By the early years of the twentieth century, however, opportunities for former slaves to accumulate power and wealth had completely evaporated.

Racial segregation was mandated in 1896 with the *Plessy v. Ferguson* decision of the United States Supreme Court, which institutionalized "Jim Crow" laws. This decision ensured that the "separate but equal" doctrine would remain national policy for almost 60 years and that Black Americans would be kept "in their place."

In the antebellum South, relations between Whites and Blacks had been dictated by laws and customs governing the acceptable conditions of slavery. From the 1600s, separating the children of slaves from their parents was permitted, but legal marriages between slaves were prohibited. Moreover, slaves were not allowed to own books, inherit money, learn to read or write, or vote. Even northern Blacks were subjected to a discriminatory set of norms. They could not vote, enter hotels or restaurants (except in the role of servants), and were segregated from Whites in formal education, trains, steamboats, church seating, and theaters (Burkey, 1971).

Jim Crow reinstated White supremacy in all aspects of everyday life. Blacks were no longer enslaved, but they were nevertheless subjected to a complex set of rules that defined them as inferior. Blacks rode in the back of public buses, drank from "colored" water fountains, waited in "colored" waiting rooms, used only "colored" public restrooms, ate in "colored" restaurants, and slept in "colored" motels. They were segregated from Whites in schools, churches, membership in unions, public accommodations, and housing.

Moreover, southern Blacks were victimized by a set of petty indignities, including prohibitions against interrace dating and marriage, against sexual relations between Black men and White women, and even against Blacks interrupting conversations between Whites. Discriminatory norms observed throughout the South required that physicians serve their White patients before their Black patients, that Blacks remove their hats when in the presence of Whites, that Black domestics enter the homes of Whites by the back door, and that Black automobile drivers yield the right-of-way to their White counterparts (Burkey, 1971).

Jobs are often but not always the primary nexus of competition between groups. In the history of American society, intergroup conflict has often taken the form of organized efforts to secure land and extend political boundaries. Hate and prejudice have developed to justify the ruthless, illegal tactics that were so frequently employed.

The experience of Mexican Americans provides a case in point. After being stereotyped by Anglos as "treacherous, childlike, primitive, lazy, and irresponsible," Mexican Americans found themselves manipulated by politicians, lawyers, and land-grabbers alike. Despite the 1848 Treaty of Guadalupe-Hidalgo, which guaranteed Mexicans the right of full citizenship, land-owning Mexican families found their titles in jeopardy and their land and cattle stolen or taken from them by fraud. Unlike their Anglo counterparts, Mexican Americans could not count on the courts for protection (Jacobs and Landau, 1971).

American Indians were severely mistreated at the hands of land-hungry White Americans who eagerly accepted the view that Indians were "treacherous and cruel savages who could never be trusted." The negative stereotype served a purpose: as long as the Indians were needed for their agricultural expertise, their military assistance, or their skill as trappers, White Americans tended to see them in a favorable light and to permit their culture to maintain itself, but when large-scale campaigns became directed toward securing the lands occupied and settled by American Indians, the negative image emerged in full force. If the central business of the "Indian savage" was to torture and slay, then the central business of the "White man" must be gradually to eliminate the "Indian savage" (Jacobs and Landau, 1971).

In some cases, the process of elimination was anything but gradual. By 1825, some 13,000 Cherokees maintained their homes in the southeastern region of the United States. They occupied seven million acres of land, owned prosperous farms, and were at peace. This situation was radically altered by the discovery of gold in the hills of Georgia. To gain possession of the rich Cherokee-owned lands, Georgia legislature, President Andrew Jackson, the United States Congress, the Supreme Court, and the military found it "necessary" to drive the Cherokees beyond the Mississippi. In the Cherokee removal of 1838, this group of American Indians were rounded up and taken away, their homes were burned, their property was seized, many were herded into stockades, and thousands died. Such thinking on the part of White Americans also led to the passage of the Dawes General Allotment Act of 1887, which took two-thirds (90 million acres) of the tribal lands previously granted to American Indians by treaty (Berry, 1965).

It isn't only the dominant group in a society that comes in conflict with the members of minorities. Throughout the history of the United States, impoverished groups have frequently competed with one another for neighborhoods, jobs, businesses, and status. As shown dramatically in the aftermath of the Rodney King episode in 1991, the recent influx of newcomers from Latin America and Asia has vastly changed the complexion of intergroup conflict in America. King, a 25-year-old Black American, was stopped while speeding down a highway in the San Fernando Valley. A local resident recorded King being repeatedly kicked and beaten by police officers and the video telecast on news programs around the country. Millions of Americans thought the police response used "excessive force."

In April 1992, when the four White police officers involved were acquitted by a predominantly White jury, many Americans were shocked and angered. Blacks were particularly outraged, considering the "police brutality" they had observed as an act of racism that was whitewashed by a racially biased jury (Levin and Thomas, 1997). Violent demonstrations broke out around the country. In Los Angeles, three days of rioting resulted in 58 deaths, 2400 injuries, $717 million in damages, and 11,700 arrests (Abelmann and Lie, 1995).

Many people likened the Los Angeles riots to the 1965 civil disturbances in Watts, which involved mostly Black Americans and resulted in numerous deaths and injuries and almost 4000 arrests. Yet, the 1992 Los Angeles riots were, in important respects, very different from Watts. The 1965 riots had been essentially Black against White. The Los Angeles riots were, by contrast, truly multi-ethnic, involving not only Blacks and Whites but also Latinos and Asians. One of the accused police officers was partially of Latino heritage; more than half of those arrested by the police were Latinos. Moreover, the majority of the more than 3000 Korean American companies in Los Angeles were damaged, the dollar amount totaling some $350 million (Kim, 1999; Abelmann and Lie, 1995).

In the 1965 riots, many of the businesses destroyed by rioters were owned by Jews. By 1992, merchants of Asian descent monopolized the local area; they were Korean Americans who had bought deteriorating businesses in Black and Latino neighborhoods. For the most part, their small shops and stores were family-owned and -run. The image of Korean merchants, like the image of Jewish merchants before them, was that of outsiders who were prospering at the expense of the Black and Latino communities. Although Asian Americans had absolutely no part in creating impoverished neighborhoods, they became scapegoats for expressing the frustrations of Black Americans against White Americans (Abelmann and Lie, 1995).

By examining the racial composition of the Los Angeles riots of 1992, we can learn a good deal about the changing conditions under which hate and prejudice are expressed in the United States. For one thing, we see that definitions of racism that neatly fit only the situation of Black and White relations during the 1960s and 1970s have lost much of their relevance to our understanding of race relations in the United States today. For decades, power was treated as a commodity that Whites possessed and Blacks only wanted. Whites had it all and Blacks had none of it. In this absolutistic way of thinking, racism equaled prejudice plus power. Thus, only Whites possessed both of the characteristics necessary to be racists, while Blacks were merely prejudiced (Tatum, 1997).

The foregoing conception may have fit the circumstances of Black–White relations traditionally, but it seems more realistic in contemporary America to consider group variations in power as being a matter of degree rather than in kind (Levin and Levin, 1982; Willie, 1996). Clearly, some groups (e.g., White men) have immensely more economic power than do other groups (e.g., people of color and women). Yet, no one group has absolute power in every respect. Individuals within even a relatively powerless group in economic terms can make their presence felt in a negative way as individuals. In 1992 Los Angeles, for example, Latinos and Black Americans as a group certainly had far less economic clout than their White neighbors, but they were still able to impose their will physically against those of their Korean American neighbors who were put out of business during the melee.

Focusing almost exclusively on Black versus White, the traditional model of intergroup conflict rightly emphasized prejudice against Black Americans as a central problem in our society. Even then, of course, the degree of economic power varied, but by ethnic group (there has long been intense and pervasive competition for scarce resources among White Ethnic Groups—Italian, Irish, Jewish, Polish, and so on) who left their homelands in Europe to make a go of it in the United States. But the new mix has become even more complex, based, as it is, on differences not in ethnic but racial characteristics. Although Europeans differed in learned cultural characteristics such as language, dress, and religious rituals, they were, for the most part, White and so didn't cross racial boundaries. The new mix introduces the added complexity of racial divisions, always a thorny issue for Americans to resolve (Parillo, 2005).

The incredible complexity of racial issues facing the United States in the early twenty-first century is represented in the recent history of affirmative action policies in higher education. Between 1970 and the mid-1980s, the number of Asian Americans attending colleges and universities dramatically increased, while enrollments of other minorities, especially of Blacks and American Indians, flattened out and then declined (Takagi, 1998). Over the same period of time, the backlash against affirmative action also began to grow. Not coincidentally, hate incidents (both criminal acts and verbal insults) targeting Black college students were on the rise on campuses around the country (Takagi, 1998; Levin and McDevitt, 1993).

Early in the rising skepticism concerning affirmative action in higher education, it was generally argued that White students were victimized by a system that unfairly gave preferential treatment to Blacks, Latinos, American Indians, and Asians. By 1986, as the notion that Asian students were *better qualified* than Whites took hold, the argument shifted, at least temporarily, so as to identify Asians and not Whites as the primary victims of affirmative action policies intended to increase the enrollment of Blacks. In other words, Black students were regarded as being in competition with Asian students for scarce seats in institutions of higher education (Takagi, 1998).

On the other side of the issue, Asian students argued that they were victims not of policies designed to attract more Black students but of blatant anti-Asian discrimination. Some university administrators countered by suggesting that Asian students were actually overrepresented relative to their proportion in the population of the United States and that the disproportionate numbers of Asian students in the classroom threatened the enrollment of truly underrepresented groups, especially Blacks and Latinos and also Whites. From this viewpoint, Asian students were depicted as qualified but usually less than outstanding. They were regarded as narrowly excellent only in science and math, as opposed to other students who had a much broader range of curricular and extracurricular interests and talents. In the face of increasing racial incidents, declining enroll-ments of Black Americans, greater pressure from Asian Americans to gain acceptance, and general concerns about academic standards, Asians were less often seen as deserving members of a "model minority" and more often as good but hardly outstanding students (Takagi, 1998).

Racial tensions on campuses around the country reflect a much more general trend toward intergroup conflict. Tensions between Blacks and Whites remain to be resolved, but they have been joined by escalat-ing levels of conflict involving Latinos and Asians as well as Muslims and Jews.

Education is only one important arena of conflict and competition. There have been large-scale Black–Asian and Black–Latino confronta-tions over economic resources and cultural differences in such cities as Miami; Washington, D.C.; New York; Chicago; and Los Angeles. More-over, in prisons across the country, differences between Latino and Black inmates have often been a source of large-scale group disturbances.

In the years ahead, as Latinos and Asians increasingly bid to have their share of the American pie, the complexities of race relations are likely to grow rather than diminish.

Maintaining Political Power

Competition for scarce resources often contributes to hate and prejudice between ethnic and racial groups in a society. Even more likely to raise the hostility of the masses, various minorities throughout history have been selected by the dominant group as "servants of power" who assumed an important role working for the rulers of society in their efforts to maintain and consolidate their status at the pinnacle of power. The position of Jews in seventeenth- and eighteenth-century Germany provides a case in point. The Jews held only a marginal position in the social structure of the larger German society. They had no citizenship rights and were despised and persecuted by the German people. As a result, German Jews, taken from the squalor of the ghetto, found them-selves at the mercy of the Germanic absolutist rulers who used them as instruments for maximizing their power in society. As servants of power to these rulers, court Jews became advisors, collaborators, bankers, and financiers. They supplied the armies, financed the wars, arranged for new loans, and settled debts. They came to monopolize the trade in silver, tobacco, and salt and built factories producing ribbon, cloth, silk, and vel-vet. In addition, they collected taxes and were diplomatic representatives, bankers, and financial administrators. Most importantly, Jews were confi-dants of the prince (Coser, 1972; Levin and Levin, 1982).

Renegade Christians were, like Jews, employed by fourteenth- and fifteenth-century Turkish sultans who sought to maintain and extend their power over their Muslim subjects. Taken as youth and converted to the Muslim faith, these foreign-born Christians became important human resources for the sultan's staff, serving in both civilian and military capacities as courtiers, administrators, and military officers. Renegade Christians provided Turkish rulers with a loyal and ambitious staff. Being the slaves of a single ruler as well as outsiders from the standpoint of the native-born population, they were totally dependent on the sultan, who, in turn, became freed from reliance on the support of his native Muslim population (Coser, 1972).

It should be noted that even where they are not chosen as servants of power, vulnerable and/or marginalized groups have frequently been targeted as the victims of collective displaced aggression. Instead of blaming the rulers of society for hard times, the masses redirect their hostility downward to such groups as welfare recipients, people of color, and Jews (Coser, 1972).

CONCLUSION

Much of the encouragement for hate attacks derives from the benefits that sympathizers and spectators secure from their verbal support or their passivity. On the psychological level, to the extent that they regard themselves as superior at the expense of others, individuals receive a boost to their self-esteem. Certain members of society, those who have a personality tendency to scapegoat outsiders, are especially likely to realize such gains. In addition, individuals who are intolerant of ambiguities benefit from the cultural images of various groups and depict these groups in stereotypical fashion. Even if such images are inaccurate, they structure the everyday experiences of a bigoted person, forming the impression that life is predictable and that dangerous people can be totally avoided.

Hate also has far-reaching economic and status benefits. Even the least bigoted members of the dominant group gain from the presence of despised individuals who are assigned the dirty work of society—the lowest-paying or most unpleasant tasks. In addition, hate justifies reducing or even eliminating the competition from less favored groups. Finally, the political leaders of society have taken advantage of outsiders who have little if any political clout and can be counted on to be loyal "servants of power." Certain minorities' supportive role in unpopular regimes, even if through no fault of their own, has engendered hostility among the masses.

In American society, many Whites continue to enjoy privileges that are simply not available to the members of racial minorities. White prerogatives are so deeply imbedded in our social structure that they may not be seen by those who enjoy them. Yet, not only do such racial advantages exist, but they continue to determine the support or lack of support that White Americans are willing to give to efforts toward eradicating racism (Feagin, 2000).

For society as a whole, hate may actually be thoroughly destructive. It robs its citizens of the possibility of unity and peace; it can easily escalate into full-scale ethnic warfare; it helps to create an entire range of costly social problems. Yet given the perceived and actual benefits of hate to particular individuals and groups in a society, the forces of resistance to change can be counted on to remain strong in the future.

■ ■ ■ ■ ■

CHAPTER 4

THE PRODUCTION OF REBELS, DEVIANTS, AND OTHER DECENT PEOPLE

THE POWER OF THE SITUATION

Hate is a mundane, everyday phenomenon typically embraced and practiced by ordinary people for ordinary reasons. Research in social psychology suggests that it really doesn't take much to make bigotry operational. Normal individuals who are placed in situations with specific role requirements by credible authority figures tend, with frightening determination, to play the roles to which they have been assigned. Of course, individuals also have some control over their culture; they don't passively have to conform to it, although, unfortunately, many of them do just that.

When Normal People Do Abnormally Nasty Things

A classic study by Philip Zimbardo and his associates at Stanford University (1973) may help shed light on the phenomenon of normal people doing abnormal, even horrific, things to others. Zimbardo and his colleagues turned the basement of a building on campus into a mock prison. They created a number of cells by installing bars and locks on each room and then placing a cot in each one. Twenty student volunteers, all chosen for their mature and stable personalities, were selected to participate in the study. On a purely random basis (the flip of a coin), half of the students were assigned to play the role of guards and the other half were assigned to play the role of prisoners.

The experiment actually started at the homes of the ten student prisoners. To increase the realism of the study, all of them were arrested, put in handcuffs, read their rights, and then driven to jail in police cars. They were then completely stripped, sprayed with disinfectants, issued prison uniforms, and placed into locked cells.

Everyone knew that the experiment was artificial and that it was supposed to end in two weeks. Nobody was really a prisoner; nobody was really a guard. It was pure make-believe decided by chance. Yet, after only a few days, both the prisoners and the guards were playing their roles to the hilt.

Guards were told only to keep order. Instead, they began to humiliate and embarrass the prisoners, coercing them to remain silent on command, to sing or laugh in front of the other inmates, and to clean up messes made by the guards. In some cases, the guards verbally and physically threatened and intimidated the prisoners, apparently for the purpose of asserting their authority.

The prisoners became more and more passive and compliant. In accord with the roles to which they had been assigned, the prisoners obeyed orders and accepted commands, no matter how unreasonable. They began to feel totally powerless to fight back. After only six days, four of the prisoners had to be excused from the study, having suffered serious episodes of anxiety, anger, or depression. In fact, the entire experiment was ended in less than a week when it became clear that the guards had become abusive and the prisoners were emotionally at risk.

Interviews conducted after the experiment ended were revealing. Both the prisoners and the guards told Zimbardo and his associates that they were both shocked and ashamed at how they had behaved. None of them would have predicted that they were capable of such cruelty, in the case of the guards, or obedience to authority, in the case of the prisoners. Remember that all of the student volunteers had been selected for their mature and stable personalities. Yet, they all acted according to the roles created by the structure of prison life.

Zimbardo's prison experiment indicates the incredible power of situational factors to influence normal individuals, whatever their psychological makeup, to mistreat other human beings or to obey the cruelest sort of authority. The hopeful implication of Zimbardo's findings is that it is easier to change situations than to change individual predispositions. We can often structure the experiences of society's members in such a way that blind conformity to bigoted norms of behavior is minimized and respect for diversity is more likely to prevail.

Fighting Spectatorship

At the same time, it is important to emphasize that spectatorship is all too comfortable for many individuals. In accepting hate and prejudice, whether actively or passively, the members of society are typically rewarded in both a psychological and material sense. By contrast, those relatively rare individuals who choose to violate norms of separatism, respect diversity, and fight for the rights of exploited and victimized groups are likely to suffer losses of their own.

Moreover, even well intentioned individuals who are willing to pay the price may not always act on behalf of vulnerable others who are in trouble. First, they must feel some sense of personal responsibility for the pain and suffering. It is all too easy to want to respond with help, but in light of the heavy personal cost, simply assume that someone else will surely come to the rescue (Latane and Darley, 1970).

Second, even if they are willing to risk their own security, they may still feel incompetent to proceed in any effective manner. Social scientists have discovered that those who intervene in a dangerous situation are likely to have had training in first aid, lifesaving, or police work. In addition, they tend to be exceptionally tall and heavy. These attributes give them the sense of efficacy (through training or strength) necessary to be injected into potentially hazardous situations. Good Samaritans also tend to be adventurous types who have taken other risks with their personal safety (London, 1970).

In addition, those who come to the rescue must realize that their help is actually appropriate to give. This means breaking through the cultural stereotypes and political propaganda to recognize that the members of a particular group are human beings who are worth saving. Education can be very effective here because it reduces stereotyped thinking (Selznick and Steinberg, 1969; Chickering and Reisser, 1993).

The difficulty of responding in the face of such ambiguities can be seen in Turkey's massacre of more than one million Armenians in 1915 (Staub, 1989). In a largely Muslim society, Armenians were part of a tiny Christian minority. Like other non-Muslims, including Greeks and Jews, Armenians tended to control Turkish commerce, trade, and finance. In addition, they were exempt from almost all taxes levied on the Islamic population. To make matters worse in a public relations sense, many of the industrious and intelligent Armenians had become quite successful; some were very wealthy. They soon became seen by the Turks as a devious, even parasitic, minority whose members had conspired with their enemy, Russia, against the majority Muslim population. By simply resisting repression and demanding their rights, Armenians were considered a threat. Not unlike other Christians in the region, they had been widely viewed as "cattle." But Armenians were also depicted as instruments of foreign intervention. Negative feelings toward the Armenian minority were exacerbated by a series of military losses that by 1913 had effectively eliminated the Ottoman Empire from Europe. During World War I, it suffered tremendous losses in a Russian invasion. By 1915, many of the country's Muslim majority held the Armenians responsible for Turkey's loss of power and its humiliating defeats (Staub, 1989).

The genocidal intentions of the Turkish leadership were not always clearcut and unambiguously immoral to the general population of Muslims. As in Germany's response to the Nazi holocaust, the mass murder of Armenians was justified as an effort to rid the homeland of an internal enemy that had long retarded the Empire's progress. Turkish writers of the day claimed that Armenian residents had committed acts of sabotage, subterfuge, espionage, and rioting. It was therefore necessary, they claimed, to deport the mutinous Armenians to minimize the damage they were inflicting on the dominant population of the country. The deportation turned out to be a death march for thousands of women, children, and elders who starved along the way. Turks admitted that lives had been lost, but that the number of deaths was actually much smaller than that claimed by Armenians. To this day, more than eight decades later, Turkey has never recognized that an Armenian massacre occurred, let alone that the Turkish government or people had some responsibility for perpetrating it (Staub, 1989).

INTERGROUP CONTACT

As we have seen, there are some Americans—black, white, and tan—who have given up on integration. They see efforts to bring together people of differing backgrounds as some sort of archaic strategy for assuaging liberal guilt rather than as an effective approach for reducing violence and other forms of discrimination. Those who are hopeless about getting groups together might find some kind of perverse comfort in the fact that major efforts at desegregating schools and neighborhoods over the past few decades have, in certain cases, ended in failure. In fact, there is even some evidence that desegregation sometimes actually supported and encouraged stereotyped thinking about the members of other races (Stephan, 1986).

The Impact of Competition

It is true that bringing groups together doesn't always reduce hate. As we have seen, various groups of Americans have been belittled, discredited, and harmed to the extent that they became widely considered a threat to the dominant group. Such historical accounts are supported by studies that show intergroup hostility escalating as a result of increasing intergroup contact, especially in the form of intense competition. In the area of employment, for example, White workers who compete directly with Blacks for jobs tend to express more bigoted racial attitudes than their counterparts in areas of the job market where there is little competition from Blacks (Cummings, 1980). The notion that hate depends for its motivation on the *threat* posed by another group of people may exaggerate the active and offensive position taken by the victim. Actually, it is the zero-sum contest that is threatening. Defensively, a group may resist when its land is taken by force, its women are sexually assaulted, its people are enslaved or carted off to concentration camps. But it is the fact that one group possesses something that another group desires, not the resistance itself, that increases hate and prejudice.

In a classic study, Sherif and his collaborators (1961) demonstrated the link between competition and intergroup hostility in a series of experiments that took place at an isolated summer camp for 11- and 12-year-old boys. After a period of time together, the boys attending Sherif's camp were separated into two distinct groups and then placed in different cabins. When each group of boys had been given the time to develop a strong sense of group spirit and organization, Sherif arranged for a number of intergroup encounters—a tournament of competitive zero-sum games such as football, baseball, tug-of-war, and a treasure hunt—in which one group could fulfill its goals only at the expense of the other group. The tournament began in a spirit of friendliness and good-natured rivalry, but it soon became apparent that negative intergroup feelings were emerging in full force. The members of each group began to name-call their rivals, completely turning against members of the opposing group, even members whom they had selected as "best friends" upon first arriving at the camp. Sherif's findings suggest that when the maintenance or enhancement of the status of a group depends on the continued subordination of another group, then intergroup competition will turn ugly.

Reducing Hostility Between Groups

Yet, notwithstanding the nasty turn of events following his introduction of competitive games, Sherif also showed us how we might be able to reverse the movement toward intergroup hostility so that the participants begin to see one another more as allies than opponents. Just having more contact didn't foster good feelings between groups; in fact, it only served to reinforce the hatred that boys from the two groups felt toward their competitors. But in the final stage of his study, Sherif introduced a series of *superordinate goals*, a set of objectives greatly valued by the boys in both groups, that could not be achieved without everyone working together. Thanks to Sherif's behind the scenes manipulations, the boys were forced collectively to push a bus out of the mud; pool their money to rent a movie; and repair their water supply, which had been sabotaged by the researchers. The result was dramatic: much of the intergroup hostility in the camp dissipated and new friendships flourished across group lines.

Sherif's concept of superordinate goals as a basis for improving intergroup relations has been applied to ethnically diverse elementary school classrooms in Texas and California (Aronson and Gonzalez, 1988). In these studies, students were interdependent in two ways: first, they were purposely structured around the goal of getting a good grade in the class so that when one student gained all of them gained. Second, their efforts were shared so that they worked together to achieve their goal (Brewer and Miller, 1996).

In a ground-breaking study, Aronson (Aronson and Patnoe, 1997) created what he called a *jigsaw teaching technique,* in which fifth-graders participated in a small experimental classroom. Each child was sorted into a racially integrated "learning group" and was given a piece of information she had to share with classmates in order to put the puzzle together. Not unlike Sherif's campers who worked together on shared goals, the key ingredient was that students in the learning group were forced to depend on one another to complete their group project and receive a grade. They taught one another; they shared information with one another. Cooperation rather than competition was the only way they could achieve a good grade in the course.

After using his jigsaw method for a period of six weeks, Aronson measured changes in the attitudes of students toward one another. As compared with children in traditional competitive classrooms, the fifth-graders in his jigsaw groups liked their classmates better, had more positive attitudes toward school, had better self-esteem, and performed just as well on their exams.

Pettigrew and Tropp (2000) concluded from their meta-analysis of 203 studies of intergroup contact that in the overwhelming majority (94 percent) of these studies, the investigators found an inverse relationship between contact and prejudice. Yet, as suggested in the findings of Sherif and Aronson, contact alone doesn't necessarily reduce hate. The effect of contact between groups depends on the quality of that contact.

Allport (1954) long ago suggested that intergroup contact would lead to a reduction in prejudice, but only under the following conditions: (1) when the groups in contact have equal status, (2) when group members engage in cooperative activity toward a shared goal, (3) when the interaction is personalized so that it breaks through stereotyped thinking, and (4) when the intergroup contact is supported by authorities or local norms. In more recent research, it has also been determined that the intergroup experience reduces prejudice to the extent that it provides participants with the opportunity to make friends with members of the other group (Pettigrew, 1998).

Most research into the impact of intergroup contact on prejudice has supported the notion that the good feeling that develops between cooperating friends from different groups actually generalizes in two ways. First, in many cases, it generalizes from the few immediate intimates to the entire group to which the few intimates belong. Second, individuals who come through contact to reduce their prejudice toward one outgroup seem to be more willing to interact with the members of outgroups generally. In other words, intergroup contact seems to reduce not only negative attitudes and feelings toward the cooperating group but also the general phenomenon known as *ethnocentrism.*

The Bulgarian experience provides an important illustration of the power of contact and cooperation in intergroup relations. In 1943, the citizens of this eastern European country, an ally of the Nazis, saved the lives of 50,000 Jewish citizens who awaited the trains that would have carried them to death camps. The Bulgarian king, Boris III, had already sent 11,000 Jews from occupied territories to their death, but his Bulgarian subjects would tolerate no more.

Unlike in many other European countics, Bulgarian Jews were dispersed throughout the social structure, playing important roles in a wide range of occupations apart from finance and commerce. Moreover, although maintaining their religious traditions and identity, many Jews were structurally assimilated into Bulgarian society, having intimate friends and acquaintances among their Christian and Muslim neighbors.

A grassroots community movement ensured that Bulgarian Jews would not be deported. There were protests from influential Bishops in the Bulgarian Orthodox Church and from the professional organizations of doctors, lawyers, and authors. A bill was introduced in Parliament by its vice-president to ignore Hitler's decree. And many average Bulgarian citizens chose to wear the yellow Star of David, a symbol that the law required Jewish citizens to wear in order to identify them for deportation (Comforty, 2000).

Structuring Opportunities for Cooperation

Recognizing the power of intergroup contact to bring diverse segments of the population together in peace and harmony, we simply cannot afford to leave such occasions to chance. Piecemeal efforts to create optimal contact experiences will result in trivial improvements in the overall social climate. Instead, we need more deliberately created, structured opportunities for members of society to interact optimally on a cooperative and intimate basis with people who are different (Pettigrew and Tropp, 2000).

Notwithstanding incidents of intergroup conflict that have inevitably arisen over the past several decades, the United States Army provides a model for viewing what consequences can be expected when an institution makes large-scale structural changes to integrate Blacks and Whites under optimal circumstances. Racial animosities decreased when soldiers worked together as equal status partners who depended on one another for survival (Moscos and Butler, 1996).

Not unlike the experience of Black and White soldiers, children coming from diverse racial and socioeconomic backgrounds can be brought together in a spirit of cooperation and mutual respect. Modeling itself on the highly successful Chicago Children's Choir, the Boston Children's Chorus consists of diverse youngsters, grades 2–12, from city and suburban neighborhoods and schools. They sing, perform, and receive the applause of their audiences as a unified and cohesive group. According to

Hubie Jones, the founder of the Boston Children's Chorus, many of the children develop friendships across racial and socioeconomic lines.

On college campuses around the country, resistance on the part of traditionally dominant students who feel threatened by the presence of new groups on campus has resulted in a revival of hate and bigotry. At one university on the east coast, for example, threatening hate mail was sent to numerous Black students on campus. At another, a student died after falling 60 feet when he and his friends attempted to affix a large hand-painted swastika to the roof of a campus building. At a small college in the mountain states, the gay and lesbian organization on campus was disbanded when all of its 12 members received threatening phone calls.

At least some of the influences working to separate students on campus by race, religion, national origin, sexual orientation, and disability status originate in the wider society and were present long before they matriculated. From an early age, for example, many children make their friendship choices within their own racial and religious groups. This pattern tends to continue through the college years. Still, the failure of such institutions of higher learning to adjust to the needs of a more diverse student body has also led many students on college campuses to resegregate themselves into special interest groups in which they might find the support and encouragement that are otherwise missing (Ehrlich, 1990).

Where separatism predominates on campus, it might be wise to create opportunities for leaders of segregated groups to come together, transcend their differences, and work in temporary alliances around common goals. Special-interest groups on campus—the gay and lesbian alliance, Latino center, international student association, Black student union, Vietnamese student alliance, and so on—are usually essential for providing minority students with what they require in order to stay in school but cannot seem to get from the wider campus community. At the same time, however, there should also be curricular and extracurricular opportunities for diverse students to put aside their differences temporarily and come together to cooperate in harmony and peace. At many colleges and universities, students from diverse backgrounds have organized rallies against violence, food and music festivals, and speaker series that defend or celebrate *all* of their group memberships.

With the same objective in mind, my colleague Will Holton and I teamed up to teach an experimental sociology course that took teams of undergraduate students out of the traditional classroom to provide service to the local community. Our primary objective was to broaden students' perspectives; to give them an opportunity to interact with people of different races, ethnicities, or religions; and to do so in a spirit of cooperation, civility, and good will.

Because of the quality of their personal essays and academic transcripts, 17 undergraduate students were selected to participate in our course. The majority was White, but Black, Asian, and Latino students were represented as well. Every week, each student in the course, as a member of a team, performed five hours of community service and then met together as a class for two hours to discuss related issues. In addition, students wrote logs summarizing their community service experiences for the week and a more inclusive paper at the end of the term. Our final class meeting together consisted of oral team presentations in which students summarized their community experiences and reflected on how those experiences had changed their own feelings and thinking about diversity.

The range of student reactions was as broad and varied as their agency placements, but typically they left a positive impression. Some reported initially feeling out of place when exposed to an unfamiliar situation in which they were, for the first time ever, the "racial minority." Others were fairly comfortable from the outset. Many students in our course discovered unexpected strengths among the community members they served. Richard, a young man from upstate New York, conducted empathy training as part of a conflict resolution program with racially diverse first-graders at an elementary school near Boston's Chinatown. Richard's experience changed his perspective. "Perhaps the biggest thing I noticed in working with these kids was just how little race differences matter to them," Richard said. "It is not that they don't understand that other people have different skin colors than they do; it's that they don't care. It made it so obvious to me that racial hatred is a learned thing."

Some of our students learned a good deal from being part of a project team whose members were diverse. For example, Marjorie, a biracial student who grew up in a part of Maine where there was only a tiny Jewish population, had been exposed to many anti-Jewish stereotypes. But through her partnership in a Cambridge agency with a Jewish woman from New York, she felt comfortable enough to speak with her about religion. Toward the end of the course, Marjorie remarked, "Now that I possess a better understanding of the Jewish faith and background, I am less likely to believe the stereotypes employed to discredit Jewish individuals."

Because they grew up shielded from those who are different, many of the students in our course were familiar with people from other racial and cultural groups only as the stereotypes they saw on television or in motion pictures. Their participation in community service learning provided an opportunity to interact cooperatively in a positive context with a wide range of individuals from other groups. At the same time, they were made aware of the existence of poverty and homelessness, flaws in the criminal justice system, prejudice and discrimination, and their own mortality. An unexpected advantage of our course for many of its students was to teach them that they are not at the center of the universe. As one of our students concluded after spending ten weeks working with Boston teenagers, "The greatest content of learning in this course was about myself. I was forced to explore my own prejudices and those of others like me."

FOLLOW THE LEADER

Researchers have discovered a common factor among German Christians who during World War II helped rescue the victims of their Nazi persecutors, civil rights activists of the 1950s and 1960s (called Freedom Riders), and altruistic children: the presence of someone to serve as a model of tolerance and empathy. For children, it is usually a parent who provides the strong moral leadership that leads them to accept a position of respect for diversity. In adults, this sort of leadership may derive from the work of politicians, entertainers, clergy, and journalists who use their platforms for the purpose of being exemplars for peace.

Sadly, our leaders—the people we count on to serve as role models for the rest of us—have not always provided the moral guidance necessary to inspire a reduction in hate and bigotry. Since the mid-1990s, for example, too many have espoused stereotyped views: Representative Robert Armey referred to his colleague in the House as Barney Fag (not Barney Frank); talk show host Howard Stern spoke of Arabs as "towel heads"; the late Khallid Mohammed, then spokesperson for Farrakhan's Nation of Islam, told a group of college students in New Jersey that Jews were "bloodsuckers"; John Rocker, an Atlanta Braves pitcher, made negative stereotypic remarks in a *Sports Illustrated* interview regarding immigrants, AIDS patients, welfare mothers, and New Yorkers; a CBS sportscaster referred to a Black basketball player as a "tough monkey"; Senator Vincent C. Fumo called his Pennsylvania colleague in the Senate a "faggot"; in an interview for Fox News Sunday, West Virginia Senator Robert Byrd used the term "white nigger"; a major league baseball umpire was suspended for referring to a female administrator as a "stupid Jew bitch"; two black bodybuilders accused California's governor Arnold Schwarzenegger, who at the time was running for office, of a history of making racist remarks; singer Michael Jackson left a message on the answering machine of his former advisor in which he suggests that "Jews suck . . . They're like leeches"; Senator Hillary Clinton joked that Mahatma Gandhi used to run a gas station in St. Louis; and speaking at a Strom Thurmond birthday party, Senator Trent Lott voiced his agreement with Thurmond's racist views.

Obeying Orders

As we have seen, leadership can also help determine whether human beings are willing to do harm to others. Even before Zimbardo conducted his famous prison study, social scientists had already experimented with what it takes to get normal individuals to do hideous things to other human beings. The role played by strong leadership at home, in the community, or at the national level in fostering or reducing hate and prejudice can hardly be exaggerated. In a classic study, Stanley Milgram (1965, 1974) sought to determine whether a group of normal Americans could be persuaded to give a severe electrical shock to a total stranger just because a legitimate authority figure ordered them to do so. Actually, Milgram's original intention was to take his experiment to Germany to examine what he hypothesized to be the strong role of obedience to authority in German national character, a factor that Milgram saw as having contributed to the willingness of ordinary German citizens to go along with Hitler's final solution. Amazingly, Milgram found so much obedience to authority in Connecticut that he never got to Germany!

Milgram's subjects, all residents of New Haven and all volunteers, were told that they were participating in a study of memory and that they would play the role of teacher or student on a random basis. In reality, all of them were predetermined to be "teachers" who were seated before an electronic apparatus containing a panel of switches labeled with varying degrees of voltage from 15 to 450 volts (labeled XXX). For every wrong answer offered by the "learner" (actually, a confederate of Milgram who pretended to get a shock by screaming or asking to be removed from the experiment), the "teacher" was told to punish him with a shock. As the study proceeded and the shock levels increased in intensity, the experimenter, dressed in a long White lab coat and holding a clipboard, urged reluctant subjects to comply by commanding them: "It is absolutely essential that you continue" and "You have no choice. You must go on." In this experiment, despite the screams of the learner and his appeal to be released from the study because of a heart condition, an incredible 60 percent of the volunteer subjects continued to administer a shock to the "learner" to the very end of the scale marked XXX at 450 volts.

In Milgram's original experiment, the learner was seated in an adjoining room some distance from the subject. The remoteness of the victim served to provide psychological distance from the teacher, who could more easily deny any personal responsibility for delivering the punishing responses. In a subsequent study, however, the learner was brought right into the room with and was seated immediately next to the teacher so that they were touching.

When the teacher and learner were in proximity rather than distant, only 30 percent, about half as many volunteers, were willing to administer a maximum shock at the urging of an authority figure (Rochat and Modigliani, 1995).

The lesson for our purposes is that it is usually easier to harm a stranger than an intimate—usually more comfortable to injure someone when her misery is not visible. Many ordinary, even decent, people will obey the orders of a credible authority figure to do harm to others, but especially when they are able to distance themselves from the pain and suffering of their victims. When people who are different in significant ways come together, when they get to know one another as human beings, and when they touch one another's lives in important ways, it becomes much more difficult for them to do harm to one another. This is true about Turks and Bulgarians, Serbians and Kosovars, Israelis and Palestinians, Protestants and Catholics in Northern Ireland, or Blacks and Whites in the United States.

The cultural, structural, and psychological bases for inspiring harmful behavior give to hate a resistance to change that may be difficult (albeit not impossible) to overcome. To some extent, culture is self-perpetuating, especially when it serves important psychological functions for the individuals and groups in a society. At the individual level, however, it appears that the emotional component of intergroup hostility can be reduced when intimacy and friendship between the members of different groups are encouraged (Pettigrew, 1997).

The second major lesson to be learned from Milgram's studies of obedience involves the power of a leader to persuade ordinary people to do extraordinarily evil things. Many of Milgram's subjects who obeyed and administered painful shocks were afterwards deeply conflicted about what they had done. Following the study, many of them perspired and trembled badly, displaying all of the symptoms associated with anxiety and concern. They were hardly sociopaths lacking in empathy and conscience. On the contrary, they cared very much but they also felt a pressing *obligation* to comply with the dictates of legitimate authority.

The Role of Leadership

Milgram's study indicates dramatically just how important leadership can be to ordinary citizens who are accustomed to taking orders and going along with experts in their fields. We grow up learning to trust our leaders. Americans are no less vulnerable to the possibility of escalating intergroup tensions from hate to violence. Even a single event can be seen as intolerable and deserving of retaliation by members of the victim's group. An instructive example of the escalation effect can be found in New York City's Crown Heights neighborhood, which has long had a history of hostility between its Black and Jewish residents. In August 1991, 7-year-old Gavin Cato, a Black child who lived in Crown Heights, was accidentally killed when a car driven by an Orthodox Jewish motorist jumped the curb. Black youngsters sought to retaliate by racing through the streets of Crown Heights as they shouted anti-Semitic epithets and threats. A short time later, matters really got out of control when a 29-year-old rabbinical student from Australia, who was totally unconnected to the accident, was stabbed to death. For almost a week, Blacks and Jews exchanged insulting remarks, hurled rocks and bottles at one another, and broke windows in homes and cars. Dozens more were injured (Levin and McDevitt, 1993; Levin and Rabrenovic, 2001; Levin and Rabrenovic, 2004a).

Intergroup incidents do not always escalate into the sort of warfare that occurred in Crown Heights. Under certain conditions, a tragic event may even facilitate reconciliation and cooperation between groups. In the aftermath of the vicious 1998 murder of James Byrd in Jasper, Texas, community responses were much more reasonable and patient than they had been in Crown Heights.

It might seem that just the opposite would occur—that the brutal murder of a Black resident in Jasper would more likely precipitate a melee than would the accidental death of a Black resident in Crown Heights. Yet, instead of dividing the community on racial grounds, the murder of James Byrd actually served to bring the Black and White residents of Jasper together. In the aftermath of the slaying, townspeople reported going out of their way to cross racial lines in greeting residents and feeling a new street-level friendliness toward members of the other race.

Following the trial and conviction of the first defendant, the white supremacist's father phoned the local radio station not to hurl racial accusations, but to urge townspeople to "fill the void made by this mess with love and tolerance" (Shlachter, 1999).

Just as in Crown Heights, Blacks and Whites in Jasper had not always been sympathetic toward one another. One issue that had long symbolized the community's struggle with race relations was the town's cemetery. A fence down the middle of the cemetery separated Whites buried on one side from Blacks buried on the other. After Byrd's murder, however, the town came to an agreement to integrate its cemetery. Many residents of Jasper, Black and White, joined together to pull out the posts and tear down the fence (Labalme, 1999).

In Crown Heights, mistrust and suspicion were palpable on both sides of the racial ledger. Many Black residents were convinced that the motorist who hit the Black child would get off scot free due to the perception that Jewish residents enjoyed special treatment from city officials. At the same time, Jewish residents of Crown Heights were certain that the Black mayor of New York City would do little if anything to bring the murderer of the Australian rabbinical student to justice.

In contrast, the political leaders in Jasper had strong credibility among both its Black and its White residents. Local government had long been racially integrated. Black residents, who comprised some 45 percent of the town's population, occupied the position of mayor, two of the five city council positions, and the directorship of the Deep East Texas Council of Governments. In addition, school principals and the administrator of the largest hospital were Black.

Jasper's White sheriff went out of his way to inspire confidence among Black residents in the aftermath of Byrd's slaying. Within 24 hours, he had arrested two suspects and then immediately requested the assistance of the FBI. Moreover, Jasper's local 6000-watt radio station kept residents informed in an even-handed way about developments related to the murder and the trials, ensuring that racially dangerous rumors and anxieties never had an opportunity to spread (Shlachter, 1999).

Another important difference between the racial incidents in Crown Heights and Jasper, Texas, involves their residents' degree of community identification. In Crown Heights, identification seemed primarily to be based on race ("the Black community"), religion ("the Jewish community"), or a shared sense of being part of the much larger New York City population. In this regard, the Crown Heights neighborhood was almost irrelevant. By contrast, Jasper, Texas, represented a primary source of community identity for Black and White residents alike—all of them felt a common bond that transcended racial differences. Even extremists on both sides were genuinely embarrassed by the cruelty and sadism of James Byrd's murder. They seemed to unite across racial lines against the very strong stigma imposed on their community by members of the outside world (Levin and Rabrenovic, 2004b).

It was recently announced by the U.S. Census Bureau that Latinos had officially replaced Blacks as America's largest minority (Wood, 2001). Latino politicians are expected to make significant gains in cities long dominated by Whites. What is more, in ethnically diverse cities such as Los Angeles, Latinos may fight for political offices held by other minorities, especially Blacks.

The relationships possible between Blacks and Latinos provide a model for understanding the choices that minority groups are likely to face in the future. The growing numbers of Latino voters in major cities across the country will ensure that they gain greater clout at least at the local level. Their increasing presence in cities and towns also places them in competition with other groups, ensuring that intergroup tensions at workplaces and in schools will occasionally flare.

The most important question for the future involves in which direction groups such as Latinos, Blacks, and Asians will decide to go. Will they choose to remain apart and in conflict? Or will they work together in a spirit of cooperation toward the fulfillment of a set of objectives important to both groups?

THE IMPACT OF DEVIANCE

In an early examination of conformity, Solomon Asch (1952) studied a group of eight people in a classroom situation who were asked to match the length of a line drawn on the blackboard with one of three comparison lines drawn on an index card. All judgments were made out loud and in order of seating in the room. Actually, only one participant in the Asch study was a naive subject; and he voiced his judgment after hearing several other students state theirs first. (These others were confederates of

Asch who had been instructed to respond incorrectly when asked to match the length of the lines.)

Over a number of trials with different groups, approximately one-third of the naive subjects made incorrect estimates in the direction of the inaccurate majority; in other words, about one in three conformed. But when a lone dissenter, a deviant, gave support to the naive subject by going against the majority judgment, the rate of conformity dropped dramatically to less than 6 percent. Thus, if even one spectator decides to break away from the inertia of the masses and become a rebel, she might serve as a role model for many other bystanders to imitate.

Because of the surprisingly large number of subjects in Milgram's experiment who obeyed a leader's order to punish a stranger, we might forget that about 40 percent of the volunteers in his original study did not comply. These were the rebels, the deviants, the incredibly decent and independently motivated people who, even under trying circumstances, simply (or not so simply) refused to follow the dictates of legitimate authority.

When Rebels Rebel

Very few Nazi or SS officers were known to have been rebels who defied authority by refusing to cooperate with anti-Jewish policies. Yet even limited opposition by rebellious German officials and citizens, especially during the early years of the Nazi regime when Hitler was still concerned about gaining popular support, might have effectively saved Jewish lives. For example, an important Nazi official in Denmark allowed the escape of more than 6000 Jews to Sweden by warning Danish leaders of the looming deportation of Jews and then delaying the execution of the order. Such noncompliance was as rare as it was dangerous. Instead, most citizens took the path of least resistance and conformed to the demands of the prevailing regime. German employers often went along with anti-Jewish policies, firing Jewish workers even before they were required to do so (Staub, 1989).

There are at least a few rebels on every campus in the United States. Refusing to be spectators or conformists in the area of intergroup relations, they organize rallies, demonstrations, festivals, or clubs on campus to bring students together or to protest the forces of division. In their exceptional zeal, they may also feel alone and unrecognized.

In March 2000 and again in March 2004, the Brudnick Center on Conflict and Violence at Northeastern University collaborated with the Center for the Prevention of Hate Violence at the University of Southern Maine to bring hundreds of college students to Boston for the purpose of attending a National Student Symposium where they received awards for their efforts at combating hate and prejudice on their campuses. Three hundred students representing more than 70 colleges and universities from more than 22 states plus the District of Columbia and the province of Quebec attended. All had been nominated for their good work by the dean of students on their campuses. The symposium was funded by the Safe and Drug-Free Schools Program of the United States Department of Education and the Bureau of Justice Assistance of the United States Department of Justice.

Student attendees were nominated on the basis of their work on an antihate project, for example, hate crimes awareness week at the University of California at Berkeley, an annual diversity festival at the University of Alabama, a community forum to end hate at the University of Southern Maine, a diversity action council at Ohio State University, and diversity peer education programs at State University of New York at Stonybrook and at Texas A&M University.

The symposium agenda included roundtable discussions in which students shared their successes and frustrations working on their campuses with issues around the objective of reducing hate and prejudice. In addition, they attended skill-building workshops that addressed such concerns and policies as confronting dating violence through student-led programs; improvising peacemaking through dance; addressing degrading language, slurs, and jokes; promoting tolerance through understanding; creating an antihate Web site; facing history and ourselves; reducing hate on campus through community service learning; and so on.

The many benefits of bringing together college students who work to combat hate and prejudice were overshadowed by the important twofold objective of the symposium: first, to recognize and reward such efforts and, second, to let students discover they are not alone. Even rebels like to know they have company and are appreciated by others.

The Importance of Empathy Across Groups

Self-interest continues too frequently to determine our most important concerns and issues. What do the late Christopher Reeves, Michael J. Fox, Doug Flutie, and Katie Couric have in common besides the fact that they are well-known media personalities? All four became champions of a cause only after they or a member of their family had been struck down by a catastrophic accident or illness. Each suffers or suffered—Reeves from a spinal cord injury, Fox from Parkinson's disease, Flutie from his son's autism, and Couric from her husband's death as a result of colon cancer. Each deserves a good deal of credit for channeling concern and energy into a worthy cause. But none became involved as a spokesperson for the cause until it had affected him in some very personal way. It is much more difficult to think of celebrities who have become thoroughly immersed in a disease that had not afflicted their own families (Jerry Lewis' annual telethon for muscular dystrophy may possibly be such an exception; talkshow host Don Imus' campaign to find a cure for autism is another).

In the same way, a missing ingredient in much of intergroup relations is *empathy that cuts across group lines:* the ability of an individual to feel the pain and suffering of groups to which she does not belong. A compelling but exceptional example of this sort of feeling for the victimization of another group of people is provided in the book *White Men Challenging Racism* (2003), a collection of 35 personal stories chronicling the experiences of white men who sought to combat racism and fight for social justice. More typically, however, when a Latino is victimized, hundreds of Latinos protest. When someone who is Jewish is bashed, hundreds of Jews demonstrate. When a gay person is attacked, hundreds of gays and lesbians march. Because they are viewed as having a vested interest, protestors who belong to a victim's group simply lack the credibility that a protestor from some other group, especially from the perpetrator's group, would have.

Sadly, it is more common for the people in one group to willingly accept the basic validity of stereotypes of other groups while they totally reject the nasty stereotypes of their own group. Thus, someone who is Black might be incensed to find that she is labeled lazy or intellectually inferior but find no difficulty in completely buying into the stereotype that all Jews are mercenary and devious. Someone who is Jewish might be outraged to learn he is stereotyped as evil and money-grubbing but might wholeheartedly agree with the image of Blacks as being stupid and lacking in motivation.

Individuals too frequently have great compassion for the plight of victims within their own group but not much left over for outsiders. Thus, Blacks might chastise Jews who continue to remember the Nazi holocaust and its victims. *It is amazing,* they argue. *Jews must think they have some kind of monopoly on suffering. More than 50 years have passed and they still dwell on the atrocities committed against Jews in Europe. It's time to stop living in the past and get on with their lives.* By the same token, Jews might be critical of Blacks who continue to recall the evils of slavery and Jim Crow segregation. *It is amazing,* they argue. *Blacks must think they have some kind of monopoly on suffering. More than a century has gone by, and they still dwell on the atrocities of slavery. Even Jim Crow laws have been dead for more than 35 years. It's time to stop blaming history for their lack of success and get on with their lives.*

Even the brightest and most distinguished observers can have tunnel vision when it comes to the suffering of their own group. David Horowitz (1994), who according to his fascinating autobiography, grew up in a Jewish home where Yiddish was spoken, placed advertisements in college newspapers around the country condemning the idea of paying reparations to Black Americans whose ancestors were enslaved. Sadly, his ads inspired not a discussion of the issue but divisiveness and hostility between various groups on a number of campuses. Students have protested, demonstrated, stolen newspapers, and demanded that the student editors who permitted the printing of ads be fired. At one university, on the day that Black students protested Horowitz's ad, a message referring to the 1999 mass murder at Columbine High and threatening to kill Blacks and Jews was found written on a men's room wall.

Putting aside the question of whether reparations for slavery are a good idea, it is clear that Horowitz's (2001) arguments are not totally without bias. To justify his view that Black Americans have done very well in this country, he unfairly compares the per capita income of Black Americans with Blacks living in African countries, when he should have compared the incomes of Black Americans today with what they would have earned if they had come to this country as a free people and hadn't experienced institutionalized oppression. He tries to minimize the prevalence of slavery by observing that only one White in five was a slaveholder. And he focuses on slavery as having occurred 150 years ago, but he fails to acknowledge the many decades of Jim Crow segregation (our version of Apartheid) that followed abolition. Ironically, very few Americans were talking seriously about the possibility of reparations for slavery until Horowitz brought the issue to public scrutiny through his college advertisements (Associated Press, 2001b).

On the Black side of the ledger, Derrick Bell (1992) has written a powerful analysis in which he convincingly argues the permanence of racism in American life. But when it comes to explaining the negative reaction of many Whites, including Jews, to Nation of Islam minister Louis Farrakhan's anti-Semitic, anti-Catholic, and anti-White statements, Bell argues that Farrakhan "is perhaps the best living example of a black man ready, willing, and able to 'tell it like it is' regarding who is responsible for racism in this country" (p. 118). Indeed, in comparison with his rather weak attempt to justify Farrakhan's bigoted rhetoric, Bell is more critical of Jews who "leap with a vengeance on inflammatory comments by Blacks" (p. 121).

We have seen that spectators find greater gains in embracing the bigotry of others than they do in respecting those who are different. In going along with hate and prejudice, spectators may believe that they benefit in terms of finances, friendships, or status. In many cases, they may be right. Conversely, opposition to bigotry may also be influenced by the perceived and actual benefits and costs. This gives us a clue that respect for differences also depends in some part on costs and benefits. In Nazi Germany, although admittedly few in number, there were pockets of resistance to the anti-Semitic measures instituted by Hitler's regime. Even as late as 1938, the leaders of two Bavarian villages risked paying the ultimate sacrifice by protecting local synagogues from being destroyed. Economic factors seemed to play a significant role in such decisions. Throughout southern Germany, local farmers depended on Jews who were actively involved in livestock trading and so they were largely opposed to barring Jewish traders from operating in their area. Until the end of 1937 when the Gestapo became actively involved, in only one district were Jews excluded from the livestock trade. Instead, Jewish traders in Bavaria continued to work and to maintain their friendships with local Christian farmers (Barnett, 1999).

The possibility of a coalition involving more than one vulnerable group seems to depend on their members' locating common ground. At the turn of the twentieth century, for example, White ethnic groups— Irish Americans, Italian Americans, and Jewish Americans—put aside their differences in favor of joining together in the labor movement. Shared economic interests became a basis for forming an alliance in the workforce.

During the 1950s and 1960s, Black Americans and Jewish Americans who recognized their shared vulnerability initially worked together in the civil rights movement. The coalition to a considerable extent dissipated as the interests of Blacks and Jews grew apart in response to significant social changes occurring through the 1970s and 1980s. First, Black Americans, especially those who emphasized "Black power," no longer felt it was desirable for Whites to assume leadership roles in the movement.[1] Second, Jewish Americans became predominantly middle- and upper-middle-class in their socioeconomic status, whereas large numbers of Black Americans remained mired in poverty. In addition, affirmative action goals and quotas that were seen by many Black Americans as advantageous to members of their group had been used historically as a weapon with which to deny Jewish Americans admission to colleges, law schools, and medical schools (Lerner and West, 1996).

Even those groups whose economic objectives do not seem to overlap might find common ground as the actual or potential victims of violence. Differences in socioeconomic status seem much less important when groups share a concern with survival in the face of hate. During the early years of the 1990s, for example, a disproportionate number of Black churches in southern states were burned to the ground, some by members of organized hate groups (e.g., the Ku Klux Klan) and others by teenagers and young adults who hated both Blacks and Jews and were looking for a thrill. Many Jewish organizations got involved in lending their assistance, giving their support, and making contributions for the purpose of repairing and restoring church buildings in the south.

Empathy across groups may be too rare, but it is far from nonexistent. In 1992, film-maker Jelena Silajdzic fled Bosnia-Herzegovina after

[1]The cofounder of the NAACP was White and Jewish. To understand the emerging negative reaction to this fact among Black Americans, simply imagine how feminists might have responded if leaders of the women's movement had been men.

watching her homeland deteriorate into a battlefield of ethnic violence and bloodshed. Settling into her new home in the Czech Republic, Silajdzic was appalled when she saw her adopted country's 200,000 Gypsies, or Roma, facing constant discrimination and humiliation. As in most central European nations, Gypsies in the Czech Republic have been restricted in restaurants, denied permission to swim in public pools, treated like shoplifters in stores and shops, segregated into inferior schools, and attacked by skinheads. In a recent survey of the residents of the Czech Republic, 79 percent of respondents said they would not want Roma as neighbors (Marklein, 2005).

Seeing this situation as intolerable, Silajdzic now heads an organization to publicize the plight of European Gypsies. In 2000, she was honored by the United Nations High Commissioner for Refugees with the Nansen Medal, an award given to one refugee from each continent who employs his skills in the service of others (Whitmore, 2001).

CONCLUSION

As we saw in Chapter 2, certain hate-filled individuals have been able to turn their lives around. Tom Leyden, for example, had been deeply entrenched in the Nazi skinhead movement and eventually renounced his bigoted views to become an activist for the cause of intergroup harmony. Working for the Simon Wiesenthal Center, he plays an important role in warning parents about the dangers of being exposed to organized hate groups through the Internet. Leyden's ability to make the transformation gives us clues as to how hatemongers and dabblers can be disabused of hate and prejudice. Leyden is an articulate and intelligent spokesperson. Everything that he gained by his membership in a racist skinhead group (the sense of belonging and the feeling of importance) Leyden continues to enjoy now by representing the other side of the issue. He is in great demand as a speaker and is frequently asked to air his views on national radio and television. Leyden's views find an audience of parents eager to learn from him how it is possible for their children to avoid making the same mistakes that he did.

Leyden's experiences suggest that we can reduce bigotry only to the extent that we give our youngsters healthy alternatives to hate and violence. Prejudice can be expected to decline to the extent that hatemongers, dabblers, sympathizers, and spectators are given structured opportunities to feel good about themselves, to have hope for the future, and to gain a sense of belonging without hating and hurting people who are different. Anything less than a major structural change will probably miss the mark.

The evidence from history and social science research suggests that intergroup harmony largely depends on the members of one group seeing members of another group as valuable human beings rather than as sub-human opponents. The roots of violent hatred are typically grounded in a tradition of intergroup aloofness and separatism in which the relations between groups have turned cold, bitter, and empty of empathy. One group comes to believe sincerely that its members would be better off by eliminating the members of another group.

Conversely, the violence of hate is unlikely when diverse people have developed a tradition of friendship, cooperation, and mutual respect, when the members of one group are not seen as a threat or a challenge to the opportunities enjoyed by another, and when the individuals in a group are widely regarded as making an important contribution to the well-being of society.

It would be tragic if, for the sake of short-term objectives, we were to allow the course of history to unfold without effectively intervening in a process otherwise destined for intergroup conflict and violence. For the purpose of reaching sympathizers and spectators, it may be necessary to create structured opportunities for increasing friendship and cooperation between groups whose members have traditionally been at serious odds. In the context of intergroup relations, it is distance, not familiarity, that breeds contempt.

■ ■ ■ ■ ■ ▬▬▬▬▬▬▬▬▬▬▬▬▬▬▬▬▬▬

ANTI-HATE WEBSITES

Anti-Defamation League
www.adl.org
Asian American Justice Center
www.napalc.org
Brudnick Center on Violence and Conflict
www.violencecenter.com
California Association of Human Relations Organizations
www.cahro.org/html/hate_crime_and_violence.html
Center for the Prevention of Hate Violence
www.preventinghate.org
Community Relations Service of the Department of Justice
www.usdoj.gov/crs/
Court TV's Choices and Consequences
www.courttv.com/choices/curriculum/hatecrime/
Emory Violence Studies Program
www.emory.edu/COLLEGE/VS/index.htm
Facing History and Ourselves
www.facing.org
FBI/Uniform Crime Reports
www.fbi.gov/ucr/ucr.htm#hate
Gay and Lesbian Alliance Against Defamation
www.glaad.org
Gay, Lesbian and Straight Education Network
www.glsen.org
Hate Crimes Research Network
www.hatecrime.net/
Human Rights Campaign
www.hrc.org
Leadership Conference on Civil Rights
www.civilrights.org
Leadership Education for Asian Pacifics
www.leap.org
National Association for Multicultural Education
www.nameorg.org

National Council of La Raza
www.nclr.org
National Gay and Lesbian Task Force
www.ngltf.org
National Italian American Foundation
www.niaf.org
National Urban League
www.nul.org
Native American Rights Fund
www.narf.org
Northeastern University's Center for the Study of Sport in Society
www.sportinsociety.org
Not in Our Town
www.pbs.org/niot
Parents, Family and Friends of Lesbians and Gays
www.pflag.org
Partners Against Hate
www.partnersagainsthate.org
Political Research Associates
www.publiceye.org/
Simon Wiesenthal Center
www.wiesenthal.com
Southern Poverty Law Center
www.splcenter.org

REMARKS ON SB390, HATE CRIMES LEGISLATION

BY DAN E. PONDER, JR., THURSDAY, MARCH 16, 2000

Dan Ponder is a former member of the Georgia State House of Representatives. The following speech can be found online at http://georgiasummit.org/legislative_News/Archive/2000/Ponder_txt.htm.

Thank you Mr. Speaker, Ladies and Gentlemen of the House.

I am probably the last person, the most unlikely person that you would expect to be speaking from the well about hate crime legislation. And I am going to talk about it a little differently from a lot of the conversations that have gone on thus far. I want to talk about it a little more personally, about how I came to believe what I believe.

About two weeks ago my family got together for my father's 70th birthday. It was the first time since my oldest daughter was born 19 years ago that only the children and spouses got together, no grandchildren. We stayed up until 2 o'clock in the morning talking about hate crime legislation, this very bill.

Even my family could not come to a resolution about this bill, but we did agree that how you were raised and who we are would likely influence how you would vote on this bill. So I want you to know a little bit about me, and how I came to believe what I believe.

I am a White Republican, who lives in the very southwest corner of the most ultraconservative part of this state. I grew up there. I have agricultural roots. I grew up hunting and fishing. I had guns when I was a kid. On my 12th birthday I was given that thing that so many southern boys receive, that shotgun from my dad that somehow marked me as a man.

I was raised in a conservative Baptist church. I went to a large, mostly White Southern university. I lived in and was the president of the largest, totally White fraternity on that campus. I had 9 separate great-great-great grandfathers that fought for the Confederacy. I don't have a single ancestor on all of my family lines that lived north of the Mason–Dixon line going back to the Revolutionary War. And it is not something that I am terribly proud of, but it is just part of my heritage, that not one, but several of those lines actually owned slaves. So you would guess just by listening to my background that I am going to stand up here and talk against hate crime legislation. But you see, that's the problem when you start stereo-typing people by who they are and where they came from, because I totally, totally support this bill.

I come from a privileged background, but hate has no discrimination when it picks its victims. I have a Catholic brother-in-law. My sister could not be married in their church, and his priest refused to marry them because they were of different faiths.

I have a Jewish brother-in-law. The difference in that religion has caused part of my family to be estranged from each other for over 25 years.

I was the president of the largest fraternity at Auburn University, which won an award while I was there as the best chapter in the country. Out of over 100 members, 6 of those are now openly gay. But the "lasting bond of brotherhood" that we pledged ourselves to during those idealistic days apparently doesn't apply if you should later come out and declare yourself gay.

Some of you know that my family had an exchange student from Kosovo that lived with us for six months, during the entire time of the fighting over there. When we last heard from her, her entire extended family of 26 members had not been heard from. Not one of them. They had all been killed or disappeared because of religious and ethnic differences that we cannot even begin to understand.

My best friend in high school and college roommate's parents were raised in Denmark during the war. His grandfather was killed serving in the Resistance.

For three years, that family survived because people left food on their doorstep during the middle of the night. They couldn't afford to openly give them food because they would then be killed themselves.

And to Representative McKinney, we are probably as different as two people can be in this House based on our backgrounds. But I myself have also known fear, because I am a White man that was mugged and robbed in Chicago in a Black neighborhood.

And you are right. It is a terror that never goes away. It doesn't end when the wounds heal or the dollars are replaced in your wallet. It is something that you live with the rest of your life.

But I want to tell you the real reason that I am standing here today. And this is personal, and in my five years in this House I have never abused my time in the well, and I only have two days before I leave this body, so I hope that you will just listen to this part for me.

There was one woman in my life that made a huge difference and her name was Mary Ward. She began working for my family before I was born. She was a young Black woman whose own grandmother raised my mother. Mary, or May-Mar as I called her, came every morning before I was awake to cook breakfast so it would be on the table. She cooked our lunch. She washed our clothes. But she was much more than that. She read books to me. When I was playing Little League she would go out and catch ball with me. She was never, ever afraid to discipline me or spank me. She expected the absolute best out of me, perhaps, and I am sure, even more than she did her own children. She would even travel with my family when we would go to our house in Florida during the summer, just as her own grandmother had done.

One day, when I was about 12 or 13 I was leaving for school. As I was walking out the door she turned to kiss me good-bye. And for some reason, I turned my head. She stopped me and she looked into my eyes with a look that absolutely burns in my memory right now and she said, "You didn't kiss me because I am Black." At that instant, I knew that she was right. I denied it. I made some lame excuse about it. But I was forced at that age to confront a small dark part of myself. I don't even know where it came from. This lady, who was devoting her whole life to me and my brother and sister, who loved me unconditionally, who had changed my diapers and fed me, and who was truly my second mother, that somehow she wasn't worthy of a good-bye kiss simply because of the color of her skin.

Hate is all around us. It takes shape and form in ways that are somehow so small that we don't even recognize them to begin with, until they somehow become acceptable to us. It is up to us, as parents and leaders in our communities, to take a stand and to say loudly and clearly that this is just not acceptable.

I have lived with the shame and memory of my betrayal of Mary Ward's love for me. I pledged to myself then and I repledged to myself the day I buried her that never, ever again would I look in the mirror and know that I had kept silent, and let hate or prejudice or indifference negatively impact a person's life; even if I didn't know them.

Likewise, my wife and I promised to each other on the day that our oldest daughter was born that we would raise our children to be tolerant. That we would raise them to accept diversity and to celebrate it. In our home, someone's difference would never be a reason for injustice.

When we take a stand, it can slowly make a difference. When I was a child, my father's plants had a lot of Whites and a lot of Blacks working in them.

We had separate water fountains. We had separate tables that we ate at.

Now my daughter is completing her first year at Agnes Scott College. She informed me last week that she and her roommate, who happens to be Black (they were thrown together just randomly last year as first-year students), had decided that they were going to room together again next year.

I asked her the reasons that they had decided to live together again. She said, "Well, we just get along so well together." She mentioned a couple of other reasons, but do you know what was absent? Color. She just didn't think about it.

You can make progress when you take a stand. Our exchange student, who grew up in a country where your differences absolutely defined everything about you, now lives in Dallas where a whole community of different races has embraced her and is teaching her how to accept people who are different from her and who love her.

To those that would say that this bill is creating a special class of citizen, I would say . . . Who would choose to be a class of citizen or who would choose to be gay and risk the alienation of your own family and friends and coworkers?

Who would choose to be Jewish, so that they could endure the kind of hatred over the years that led to the Holocaust and the near extinction of the Jewish people on an entire continent?

Who would choose to be Black simply so that their places of worship could be burned down or so that they could spend all their days at the back of the line? We are who we are because God alone chose to make us that way. The burdens that we bear and the problems that we are trying to correct with this legislation are the result of man's inhumanity to man.

That is hardly trying to create a special class of people.

To those that would say that we already have laws to take care of these crimes, I would say watch the repeats of yesterday's debate on the Lawmakers.

We made passionate pleas on behalf of animal rights. We talked with revulsion about cats being wired together with barbed wire. Surely, surely, Matthew Shepard's being beaten and hung up on a barbed wire fence and left to die is no less revolting. Surely our fellow man deserves no less than our pets.

Hate crimes are different. When I was a teenager, on more than one water tank, I painted "SR's of '72";. Surely no one in here is going to tell me that the words that are painted on walls that say "Kill the Jews" or a swastika or "Fags must die" or "Move the Niggers" are somehow the same as "SR's of '72". Even today, those very words make us feel uncomfortable and they should.

Surely we are not going to equate a barroom brawl or a crime of passion with a group that decides, with purpose, to get in a car and go beat up Blacks or gays or Jews without even knowing who they are.

Hate crimes are about sending a message. The cross that was burned in a Black person's yard not so many years ago was a message to Black people.

The gay person that is bashed walking down the sidewalk in midtown is a message to gay people.

And the Jews that have endured thousands of years of persecution were all being sent messages over and over again.

I would say to you that now is our turn to send a message. I am not a lawyer, I don't know how difficult it would be to prosecute this or even care.

I don't really care that anyone is ever prosecuted under this bill. But, I do care that we take this moment in time, in history, to say that we are going to send a message. The Pope is now sending a message of reconciliation to Jews and people throughout this world. Some of those crimes occurred 2000 years ago.

My wife and I have sent a message to our children that we are all God's children and that hate is unacceptable in our home.

I believe that we must send a message to people that are filled with hate in this world, that Georgia has no room for hatred within its borders. It is a message that we can send to the people of this state, but it is also a message that you have to send to yourself.

I ask you to look within yourself and do what you think is right. I ask you to vote YES on this bill and NO to hate.

REFERENCES

Abelmann, Nancy, and John Lie (1995). *Blue Dreams: Korean Americans and the Los Angeles Riots.* Cambridge, MA: Harvard University Press.

Adorno, Theodore W., Else Frankel-Brunswick, Daniel J. Levinson, and Nevitt H. Sanford (1950). *The Authoritarian Personality.* New York: Harper and Row.

Allport, Gordon W. (1954). *The Nature of Prejudice.* Reading, MA: Addison-Wesley.

American Academy of Child and Adolescent Psychiatry (2005). "Multiracial-Children," http://www.aacap.org/publications/factsfam/71.htm, accessed. April 20, 2006.

Ancheta, Angelo N. (1998). *Race, Rights, and the Asian American Experience.* New Brunswick, NJ: Rutgers University Press.

Anti-Defamation League (1988). "'JAP Baiting': When Sexism and Anti-Semitism Meet," *Special Edition of ADL Periodic Update.* New York: ADL.

——— (1995). *The Skinhead International.* New York: ADL.

——— (1997). *Vigilante Justice: Militias and Common Law Courts Wage War Against the Government.* New York: ADL.

——— (2000). *ADL Backgrounder on Anti-Semitism in the United States.* New York: ADL.

——— (2001). "Anti-Semitism and Prejudice in America." New York: ADL.

——— (2005). "Anti-Semitic Incidents at Highest Level in Nine Years." *ADL Audit* (April 4). New York: ADL.

——— (2006). "Extremists Declare 'Open Season on Immigrants; Hispanics Target of Incitement and Violence." *ADL Report* (April 24). New York: ADL.

Armas, Genaro C. (2001). "Asian-American Population Surges," *Boston Globe* (March 11), p. A2.

Aronson, Elliot, and Alex Gonzalez (1988). "Desegregation, Jigsaw, and the Mexican-American Experience." In P. Katz and D. Taylor (eds.), *Eliminating Racism: Profiles in Controversy.* New York: Plenum Publishing.

Aronson, Elliot, and Shelley Patnoe (1997). *The Jigsaw Classroom.* New York: Longman.

Asch, Solomon (1952). "Effects of Group Pressures Upon the Modification and Distortion of Judgment." In G. E. Swanson, T. M. Newcomb, and E. L. Hartley (eds.), *Readings in Social Psychology.* New York: Holt, Rinehart, and Winston.

Associated Press (1994). "Man Convicted of Hate Crime Killing" (September 16), www.nexis.com. April 22, 2006

——— (1997). "Gunshots Aimed at Home of Black Family" (June 6), www.nexis.com. April 22, 2006.

——— (2001). "U Conn Students Protest Reparations Ad" (April 21), www.nexis.com. April 22, 2006.

——— (2005). "Iran Leader Denounces Prophet Cartoons" (February 7), www.nexis.com. April 22, 2006.

Australia Immigration Visa Services (2000). "Immigration Laws" (July), http://www.migrationint.com.au/news/gabraltar/jul_2000-12mn.asp.

Australian Broadcasting Corporation (2005). "Iranian President Denies Holocaust" (December 14), http://www.abc.net.au/news/newsitems/200512/s1531177.htm.

Barnett, Victoria J. (1999). *Bystanders: Conscience and Complicity During the Holocaust.* Westport, CT: Praeger.

Beck, Aaron T. (1999). *Prisoners of Hate: The Cognitive Basis of Anger, Hostility, and Violence.* New York: HarperCollins.

Belkin, Douglas (2001). "Anti-Semitic Beliefs Revealed in Death," *Boston Globe* (January 7), p. B7.

Bell, Derrick (1992). Faces *at the Bottom of the Well: The Permanence of Racism.* New York: Basic Books.

Beller, Steven (1997). "'Pride and Prejudice' or 'Sense and Sensibility'?" In D. Chirot and A. Reid (eds.), *Essential Outsiders*. Seattle: University of Washington Press.

Bellisfield, Gwen (1972–1973). "White Attitudes Toward Racial Integration and the Urban Riots of the 1960's," *Public Opinion Quarterly* (Winter): 579–584.

Bem, Daryl J. (1970). *Beliefs, Attitudes, and Human Affairs*. Belmont, CA: Brooks/Cole.

Berrill, Kevin (1992). "Anti-Gay Violence and Victimization in the United States: An Overview." In G. Herek and K. Berrill (eds.), *Hate Crimes: Confronting Violence Against Lesbians and Gay Men*. Newbury Park, CA: Sage Publications.

Berry, Brewton (1965). *Race and Ethnic Relations*. Boston: Houghton Mifflin.

Billig, Michael, and Henri Tajfel (1973). "Social Categorization and Similarity in Intergroup Behavior," *European Journal of Social Psychology* 3:27–52.

Blakeslee, Spencer (2000). *The Death of American Antisemitism*. Westport, CT: Praeger.

Blascovich, James, Natalie Wyer, L. A. Swart, and John Kibler (1997). "Racism and Racial Categorization," *Journal of Personality and Social Psychology* 72:1364–1372.

Bonacich, Edna (1972). "A Theory of Ethnic Antagonism: The Split Labor Market," *American Sociological Review* (October): 547–559.

Bonds, Maria, and Sally Stoker (2000). *Bully-Proofing Your School*. Longmont, CO: Sopris West.

Borgeson, Kevin (in press). "A Typology of Aryan Nations Members." *American Behavioral Scientist*.

Brewer, Marilynn B., and Norman Miller (1996). *Intergroup Relations*. Ann Arbor, MI: Brooks/Cole.

Brigham, Carl (1923). *A Study of American Intelligence*. Princeton, NJ: Princeton University Press.

Brink, William, and Louis Harris (1964). *The Negro Revolution in America*. New York: Simon and Schuster.

Brink, William, and Louis Harris (1967). *Black and White*. New York: Simon and Schuster.

Brook, Kevin Alan (1999). *The Jews of Khazaria*. Northvale, NJ: Jason Aronson.

Brown, Roger (1986). *Social Psychology: The Second Edition*. New York: The Free Press.

Brown, Tony (1995). *Black Lies, White Lies*. New York: William Morrow.

Browning, Christopher R. (1992). *Ordinary Men*. New York: HarperPerennial.

Brustein, William (1996). *The Logic of Evil*. New Haven, CT: Yale University Press.

————, and Ryan King (forthcoming). "AntiSemitism in Europe Before the Holocaust." In K. Beohnke, D. Fuss, and J. Hagan (eds.), *Fremdenfeindlichkeit, Rechtsextremeismus, Jugendgewalt: Internationale Soziologische und Psychologische Perspektiven*. Weinheim: Juventa.

Bureau of Justice Assistance (1997). *A Policy Makers Guide to Hate Crimes*. Washington, D.C.: U.S. Government Printing Office.

Burkey, Richard M. (1971). *Racial Discrimination and Public Policy in the United States*. Lexington, MA: Heath.

Campbell, Angus (1971). *White Attitudes Toward Black People*. Ann Arbor, MI: University of Michigan Press.

CBS4Boston (2006). "Manhunt Continues for New Bedford Shooting Suspect" (February 2), http://cbs4boston.com/topstories/local_story_033062737.html.

Chesler, Phyllis (2003). *The New Anti-Semitism*. San Francisco: Jossey-Bass.

Chickering, A. W. and L. Reisser (1993). *Education and Identity* . San Francisco: Jossey-Bass.

CNN (2000). "True Believers; Hot Rocks; Breach of Faith" (August 6), www.nexis.com.

———— (2001). "Hate Crime Reports Up in Wake of Terrorist Attacks" (September 17), www.nexis.com.

Comer, James P. (1972). *Beyond Black and White*. Chicago: Quadrangle.

Comforty, Jacky (2000). *The Optimists*. Evanston, IL: Comforty Media Concepts.

Coser, Lewis A. (1972). "The Alien as a Servant of Power: Court Jews and Christian Renegades," *American Sociological Review* (October): 574–581.

Crocker, Jennifer, and Brenda Major (1989) "Social Stigma and Self Esteem: The Self Protective Properties of Stigma," *Psychological Review* 96:608–630.

Cummings, S. (1980). "White Ethnics, Racial Prejudice and Labor Market Segmentation," *American Sociological Review* 85:938–950.

Dalesio, Emery P. (2006). "Was Ex-Student's SUV Attack a Hate Crime?" Associated Press (March 4).

Deane, Claudia, and Darryl Fears (2006). "Negative Perception of Islam Increasing," *Washington Post* (March 9), p. 1.

DeMillo, Andrew (2000). "Student Says Harassment Haunted Her," *Seattle Times* (August 5), p. A11.

Dimont, Max I. (1962). *Jews, God, and History.* New York: Signet.

Ehrlich, Howard (1972). *The Social Psychology of Prejudice.* New York: Wiley.

——— (1990). *EthnoViolence on College Campuses.* Baltimore: National Institute Against Prejudice and Violence.

Elder, Larry (2000). *The Ten Things You Can't Say in America.* New York: St. Martin's Press.

Esposito, John L. (2006). "Muslims and the West: A Culture War?" Gallup News Service (February 13).

Ezekiel, Raphael S. (1995). *The Racist Mind: Portraits of American NeoNazis and Klansmen.* New York: Viking.

Feagin, Joe R. (2000). *Racist America: Roots, Current Realities, and Future Reparations.* New York: Routledge.

———, and Hernan Vera (1995). *White Racism.* New York: Rutledge.

FBI (2005). *Hate Crime Statistics.* Washington, D.C.: U.S. Government Printing Office.

Fein, H. (1979). *Accounting for Genocide: National Responses and Jewish Victimization During the Holocaust.* New York: The Free Press.

Finn, Peter (2000). "NeoNazis Spreading Hate Chat from US," *Boston Globe* (December 22), p. A19.

——— (2002). "A Turn from Tolerance: Anti-Immigrant Movement in Europe Reflects Post–Sept 11 Views on Muslims," *Washington Post* (March 29), p. A1.

Fishbein, Harold D. (1996). *Peer Prejudice and Discrimination.* Boulder, CO: Westview Press.

Fiske, Susan T., and Steven L. Neuberg (1990). "A Continuum of Impression Formation, from Category-Based to Individuating Processes." In M. P. Zanna (ed.), *Advances in Experimental Social Psychology* (Vol. 23). New York: Academic Press.

Fletcher, Michael A. (2001). "Anti-Black Hate Mail Roils Penn State," *Boston Globe* (May 3), p. A21.

FNC (2000). "Special Report," (August 9) www.nexis.com.

Fox, James, and Jack Levin (2006). *The Will to Kill: Explaining Senseless Murder.* Boston: Allyn and Bacon.

Frankel, Glenn (2003). "For Jews in France, a 'Kind of Intifada'; Escalation in Hate Crimes Leads to Soul-Searching, New Vigilance," *Washington Post* (July 16), p. A1.

Franklin, John Hope, and Isidore Starr (1967). *The Negro in 20th Century America.* New York: Vintage.

Galton, Francis (1883). *Inquiries into Human Faculty and Its Development.* London: Macmillan.

Gambino, Richard (1977). *Vendetta.* New York: Doubleday.

Genovese, Eugene D. (1969). *The World the Slaveholders Made.* New York: Pantheon.

Gilbert, G. M. (1951). "Stereotype Persistence and Change Among College Students," *Journal of Abnormal and Social Psychology* (April): 245–254.

Goldhagen, Daniel Jonah (1996). *Hitler's Willing Executioners: Ordinary Germans and the Holocaust.* New York: Basic Books.

Goodstein, Laurie (1996). "Report Cites Harassment of Muslims," *Washington Post* (April 20), p. A3.

Gordon, Danielle, and Natalie Pardo (1997). "Hate Crimes Strike Changing Suburbs," *Chicago Reporter* (September), p. 1.

Green, Donald P., Dara Z. Strolovitch, and Janelle S. Wong (1997). "Defended Neighborhoods, Integration, and Hate Crime," unpublished manuscript, Institution for Social and Policy Studies. New Haven, CT: Yale University.

Gullo, Karen (2001). "US Report Links Race, Force Used by Police," *Boston Globe* (March 11), p. A3.

Halpern, Thomas, and Brian Levin (1996). *The Limits of Dissent: The Constitutional Status of Armed Civilian Militias.* Amherst, MA: Aletheia Press.

Hamm, Mark S. (1994). *Hate Crime: International Perspectives on Causes and Control.* Cincinnati: Anderson.

Harlow, Caroline Wolf (2005). *Hate Crime Reported by Victims and Police.* Bureau of Justice Statistics Special Report (November). Washington, D.C.: Bureau of Justice Statistics.

Harris, Hamil R. and Paul Farhi (2004). "Debate Continues as Cosby Again Criticizes Black Youths," *Washington Post* (July 3), p. A1.

Harris Interactive (2005). "Labour Enjoys a 13-Point Lead in Party Identification, but Tories More Likely to Vote" (May 2), www.nexis.com.

Harris, Marvin (1964). *Patterns of Race in the Americas.* New York: Walker.

Healy, Patrick (2001). "Student Killed in Fall Was Carrying Swastika," *Boston Globe* (May 3), p. B5.

Helm, Toby (2001). "Young Germans See 'Good Side' to Nazis," *Daily Telegraph* (February 8), p. 17.

Herrnstein, Richard J. (1971). "I.Q.," *The Atlantic* (September): 43–64.

———, and Charles Murray (1994). *The Bell Curve: Intelligence and Class Structure in American Life.* New York: The Free Press.

Hilberg, Raul (1992). *Perpetrators, Victims, Bystanders: The Jewish Catastrophe 1933–1945.* New York: HarperCollins.

Holian, Timothy J. (1998). *The German Americans and World War II.* New York: Peter Lang.

Horowitz, David (1994). *Radical Son.* New York: Touchstone Books.

——— (2001). "Ten Reasons Why Reparations for Blacks Is a Bad Idea for Blacks—and Racist Too," *FrontPageMagazine.Com* (January 3), www.nexis.com.

Hummel, Jeffrey (1987). "Not Just Japanese Americans," *The Journal of Historical Review* 7 (3, Fall): 285.

Hyman, Herbert H., and Paul B. Sheatsley (1956). "Attitudes Toward Desegregation," *Scientific American* 195:35–39.

——— (1964). "Attitudes Toward Desegregation," *Scientific American*, 211:16–23.

Iganski, Paul, and Barry Kosmin (2003). *A New Anti-Semitism? Debating Judeophobia in 21st-Century Britain.* London: Profile Books and the Institute for Jewish Policy Research.

Iganski, Paul, Vicky Kielinger, and Susan Paterson (2005). *Hate Crimes Against London's Jews.* London: Institute for Jewish Policy Research.

Jacobs, James B., and Jessica S. Henry (1996). "The Social Construction of a Hate Crime Epidemic," *The Journal of Criminal Law and Criminology* (Winter): 366–391.

Jacobs, James B., and Kimberly A. Potter (1997). "Hate Crimes: A Critical Perspective." In M. Tonry (ed.), *Crime and Justice: A Review of Research.* Chicago: University of Chicago Press.

——— (1998). *Hate Crimes: Criminal Law and Identity Politics.* New York: Oxford University Press.

Jacobs, Paul, and Saul Landau, with Eve Pell (1971). *To Serve the Devil* (Vol. 1). New York: Vintage.

Janofsky, Michael (1997). "Under Siege, Philadelphia's Criminal Justice System Suffers Another Blow," *New York Times* (April 10), p. A14.

Jenness, Valerie, and Kendal Broad (1997). *Hate Crimes: New Social Movements and the Politics of Violence.* New York: Aldine De Gruyter.

Jenness, Valerie, and Ryken Grattet (2004). *Making Hate a Crime: From Social Movement to Law Enforcement.* New York: Russell Sage Foundation.

Jones, Jeffrey M. (2005). "Nurses Remain Atop Honesty and Ethics List," *Gallup News Service* (December 5), www.gallup.com May 1, 2006.

Kamin, Leon (1973). "War of IQ: Indecisive Genes," *Intellectual Digest* (December): 22–23.

Karl, Jonathan (1995). *The Right to Bear Arms.* New York: Harper.

Karlins, Marvin, Thomas L. Coffman, and Gary Walters (1969). "On the Fading of Social Stereotypes: Studies in Three Generations of College Students," *Journal of Personality and Social Psychology* (September): 1–16.

Katz, David, and Kenneth Braly (1933). "Racial Stereotypes of One Hundred College Students," *Journal of Abnormal and Social Psychology* (October–December): 280–290.

Katz, Fred E. (1993). *Ordinary People and Extraordinary Evil.* Albany: State University of New York Press.

Keen, Sam (1988). *Faces of the Enemy.* New York: Harper and Row.

Kim, Kwang Chung (1999). *Koreans in the Hood.* Baltimore: Johns Hopkins University Press.

Klanwatch Intelligence Report (1997). "Two Years After: The Patriot Movement Since Oklahoma City," (Spring) pp. 18–20.

Kochiyama, Yuri (2001). "Then Came the War." In J. Ferrante and P. Browne, Jr. (eds.), *The Social Construction of Race and Ethnicity in the United States,* 2nd ed. Upper Saddle River, NJ: Prentice Hall.

Kovel, Joel (1971). *White Racism: A Psychohistory.* New York: Vintage Books.

Labalme, Jenny (1999). "Discussion Focuses on Hate Crimes." *Indianapolis Star* (November 17), p. B1.

La Gumina, Salvatore J. (1973). *Wop!* San Francisco: Straight Arrow.

Lamy, Philip (1996). *Millennium Rage.* New York: Plenum Press.

Lane, Roger (1997). *Murder in America: A History.* Columbus, OH: Ohio State University Press.

Langer, Elinor (1990). "The American NeoNazi Movement Today," *The Nation* (July 16/23), pp. 82–107.

Larson, Susan (2000). "Essays Explore, Illuminate Creole Culture," *Times-Picayune* (August 26), p. 3.

Latane, Bibb, and John M. Darley (1970). *The Unresponsive Bystander.* New York: Appleton-Century-Crofts.

Laue, Christine (2000). "A Wave of Student Activities in Suburban Omaha and Nationwide Seeks Harassment Protections," *Omaha World Herald* (May 7), p. 1.

Lawrence, Charles (1987). "The Id, the Ego and Equal Protection: Reckoning with Unconscious Racism," *Stanford Law Review* 39:317–323.

Lawrence, Frederick M. (1999). *Punishing Hate: Bias Crimes Under American Law.* Cambridge, MA: Harvard University Press.

Lazare, Bernard (1894). *AntiSemitism: Its History and Causes.* Lincoln: University of Nebraska Press, English translation, 1995.

Lee, Yueh-Ting, Lee Jussim, and Clark McCauley (1995). *Stereotype Accuracy: Toward Appreciating Group Differences.* Washington, D.C.: American Psychological Association.

Leparmentier, Arnaud (2000). "German Racist Killers Get Long Jail Terms," *Manchester Guardian Weekly* (September 13), p. 33.

Lerner, Michael, and Cornel West (1996). *Jews and Blacks.* New York: Plume Books.

Levin, Brian (1992–1993). "Bias Crimes: A Theoretical and Practical Overview," *Stanford Law and Policy Review* (Winter): 165–171.

Levin, Jack (1996). "Teenagers Burn Churches," *Boston Globe* (December 12), Focus section, p. E2.

——— (1997a). "Visit to a Patriot Potluck," *USA Today* (March 1), p. A6.

——— (1997b). "N. Irish Racialize 'The Troubles,'" *Boston Herald* (July 13), p. 22.

———, and James A. Fox (1991). *Mass Murder: America's Growing Menace.* New York: Berkley Books.

Levin, Jack, and William J. Levin (1982). *The Functions of Discrimination and Prejudice.* New York: Harper and Row.

——— (1988). *The Human Puzzle.* Belmont, CA: Wadsworth.

Levin, Jack, and Jack McDevitt (1993). *Hate Crimes: The Rising Tide of Bigotry and Bloodshed.* New York: Plenum.

——— (1995a). "The Research Needed to Understand Hate Crime," *Chronicle of Higher Education* (August 4), p. B12.

——— (1995b). "Landmark Study Reveals Hate Crimes Vary Significantly by Offender Motivation," *Klanwatch Intelligence Report* (August), p. 79.

——— (1995c). "Messages of Intolerance," *Boston Globe* (April 27), p. 9.

——— (2002). *Hate Crimes Revisited: America's War Against Those Who Are Different.* Boulder, CO: Westview Press.

Levin, Jack, and Monte Paulsen (1999). *Encyclopedia of Human Emotions* (Vol. 1). New York: Macmillan Reference.

Levin, Jack, and Gordana Rabrenovic (2001). "Hate Crimes and Ethnic Conflict: An Introduction," *American Behavioral Scientist* 45(4): 574–588.

———. (2004a). "Preventing Ethnic Violence: The Role of Interdependence," *The Psychology of Ethnic Conflict.* Edited by Yueh-Ting Lee. Westport, CT: Greenwood Press.

———. (2004b). *Why We Hate.* Amherst, NY: Prometheus Books.

———. (2006). "Give Us Still Your Masses . . ." *Boston Herald* (April 7), p. 25.

Levin, Jack, and Alexander R. Thomas (1997). "Experimentally Manipulating Race: Perceptions of Police Brutality in an Arrest." *Justice Quarterly* (September): 577–585.

Lewis, Oscar (1968). "The Culture of Poverty." In D. P. Moynihan (ed.), *On Understanding Poverty.* New York: Basic Books.

Lifton, Robert (1961). *Thought Reform and the Psychology of Totalism.* New York: W.W. Norton.

Locksley, Anne, Vilma Ortiz, and Christine Hepburn (1980). "Social Categorization and Discriminatory Behavior: Extinguishing the Minimal Intergroup Discrimination Effect," *Journal of Personality and Social Psychology* 39(7): 73–83.

Logan, Rayford (1954). *The Betrayal of the Negro.* New York: Collier.

London, P. (1970). "The Rescuers: Motivational Hypotheses About Christians Who Saved Jews from the Nazis." In J. Macauley and L. Berkowitz (eds.), *Altruism and Helping Behavior.* New York: Academic Press.

Ludwig, Jack (2000). "Perceptions of Black and White Americans Continue to Diverge Widely on Issues of Race Relations in the U.S.," *Gallup News Service* (February 28).

Macdonald, Andrew (1978). *The Turner Diaries.* New York: Barricade Books.

Marklein, Mary Beth (2005). "European Effort Spotlights Plight of the Roma," *USA Today* (February 2), p A6.

McClintock, Michael (2005). *Everyday Fears: A Survey of Violent Hate Crimes in Europe and North America.* New York: Human Rights First.

McDevitt, Jack, Jack Levin, and Susan Bennett (2002), "An Updated Typology of Hate Crime Motivations," *Journal of Social Issues* 58:303–317.

McWhorter, John H. (2000). *Losing the Race: Self Sabotage in Black America.* New York: The Free Press.

——— (2005). *Winning the Race: Beyond the Crisis in Black America.* New York: Gotham Books.

Merton, Robert K. (1957). *Social Theory and Social Structure.* New York: The Free Press.

Milgram, Stanley (1965). "Some Conditions of Obedience and Disobedience to Authority," *Human Relations* 18:57–75.

——— (1974). *Obedience to Authority: An Experimental View.* New York: Harper and Row.

Moscos, Charles, and John Butler (1996). *All That We Can Be: Black Leadership and Racial Integration in the Army Way.* Basic Books: New York.

Moynihan, Daniel P. (1965). *The Negro Family: The Case for National Action.* Washington, D.C.: U.S. Government Printing Office.

Myrdal, Gunnar (1944). *An American Dilemma.* New York: Harper and Row.

Not in Our Town II (1996). Public Broadcasting System.

National Conference for Community and Justice (2000). *Taking America's Pulse*

II: Survey of Intergroup Relations in the United States. New York: NCCJ.

National Journal Group, Inc. (2000). "Lieberman: Dallas NAACP Chapter Pres. Gone After 'Jew' Comment" (August 10), www.nexis.com.

Newport, Frank (1999). "Racial Profiling Is Seen as Widespread, Particularly Among Young Black Men," *Gallup News Service* (December 9).

Nickerson, Colin (2006). "Racial Attacks in Germany Stir World Cup Fear," *Boston Globe* (April 24), pp. 1, 8.

Noel, Donald L. (1968). "A Theory of the Origin of Ethnic Stratification," *Social Problems* (Fall): 157–172.

Office of Juvenile Justice and Delinquency Prevention (1996). *Report to Congress on Juvenile Hate Crime.* Washington, D.C.: U.S. Government Printing Office.

Oliver, Christian (2006). "Cartoon Crisis Deepens as Muslim Fury Spreads," Reuters, http://today.reuters.com/misc/PrinterFriendlyPopup.aspx?type+topNews&storyID=uri:2006-02 07T1.

Olzak, Susan, Suzanne Shanahan, and Elizabeth H. McEneaney (1996). "Poverty, Segregation, and Race Riots: 1960 to 1993," *American Sociological Review* (August): 590–613.

Osborne, Jason (1995). "Academics, Self Esteem, and Race: A Look at the Underlying Assumptions of the Disidentification Hypothesis," *Personality and Social Psychology Bulletin* 21:449–455.

Parillo, Vincent N. (2005). *Strangers to These Shores.* Boston: Allyn and Bacon.

Patriot Fax Network (1996). "Origin of Khazarians."

Patterson, Orlando (1998). *Rituals of Blood.* New York: Basic Civitas.

Pearce, Diana M. (1979). "Gatekeepers and Homeseekers: Institutional Patterns in Racial Steering," *Social Problems* (February): 325–342.

Perry, Barbara (2003). "Where Do We Go from Here? Researching Hate Crime," *Internet Journal of Criminology*, www.internetjournalofcriminology.com.

Petroni, Frank A. (1972). "Adolescent Liberalism—The Myth of a Generation Gap," *Adolescence* (Summer): 221–232.

Pettigrew, Thomas F. (1964). *A Profile of the Negro American.* New York: Van Nostrand Reinhold.

——— (1997). "The Affective Component of Prejudice: Empirical Support for the New View." In S. A. Tuch and J. K. Martin (eds.), *Racial Attitudes in the 1990s: Continuity and Change.* Westport, CT: Praeger.

——— (1998). "Intergroup Contact Theory," *Annual Review of Psychology* 49:65–85.

———, and Linda R. Tropp (2000). "Does Intergroup Contact Reduce Prejudice? Recent Meta Analytic Findings." In S. Oskamp (ed.), *Reducing Prejudice and Discrimination.* Mahwah, NJ: Lawrence Erlbaum Associates.

Pratto, Felicia (1996). "Sexual Politics: The Gender Gap in the Bedroom, the Cupboard, and the Cabinet." In D. M. Buss and N. M. Malamuth (eds.), *Sex, Power, Conflict: Evolutionary and Feminist Perspectives.* New York: Oxford University Press.

———, James Sidanius, L. M. Stallworth, and B. F. Malle (1994). "Social Dominance Orientation: A Personality Variable Predicting Social and Political Attitudes," *Journal of Personality and Social Psychology* 67:741–763.

Quanty, Michael B., John A. Keats, and Stephen G. Harkins (1972). "Prejudice and Criteria for Identification of Ethnic Photographs," *Journal of Personality and Social Psychology* 32:449–454.

Radler, Melissa (2001). "ADL: Antisemitism up 49% in NYC," *Jerusalem Post* (March 22), p. 5.

Rayburn, Jim (1999). "Cross Burner Found Guilty," *Deseret News* (September 1), p. B1.

Religion News Service (2005). "In Brief," *Washington Post* (November 19), p. B9.

Reuters (2001). "Feud with Bully Eyed in Pa. Shooting," *Boston Globe* (March 9), p. A5.

Robertson, Tatsha, and Ross Kerber (2000). "History Unchained," *Boston Sunday Globe* (August 6), p. B12.

Rochat, Francois, and Andre Modigliani (1995). "The Ordinary Quality of Resistance: From Milgram's Laboratory to the Village of Le Chambon," *Journal of Social Issues* 5:195–210.

Rodriguez, Cindy (2001). "Latinos Surge in Census Count," *Boston Globe* (March 8), p. 1.

Rokeach, Milton (1952). "Attitude as a Determinant of Recall," *Journal of Abnormal and Social Psychology*, 47:482–488.

Rosenblum, Mort (2003). "Unease Grows Among Europe's Jews," *Washington Post* (December 14), p. A29.

Rosenwald, Michael (2002). "Many Teens Silent on Hate Crimes, Study Finds," *Boston Globe* (January 28), p. B2.

Rosnow, Ralph L. (1972). "Poultry and Prejudice," *Psychology Today* (March): 53–56.

Roth, Alex (2001). "Teenager Charged in Rampage Speaks Out," *San Diego Union Tribune* (February 1), p. B1.

Rothbard, M., M. Evans, and Solomon Fulero (1979). "Recall for Confirming Events: Memory Processes and the Maintenance of Social Stereotyping," *Journal of Experimental Social Psychology* 15:343–355.

Rowan, Carl T. (1996). *The Coming Race War in America.* Boston: Little, Brown, and Company.

Rushton, J. Philippe (2001). *Race, Evolution, and Behavior: A Life History Perspective.* Port Huron, MI: Charles Darwin Research Institute.

Russell, Katheryn K. (1998). *The Color of Crime.* New York: New York University Press.

Ryan, William (1971). *Blaming the Victim.* New York: Vintage.

Saad, Lydia (2005). "Gay Rights Attitudes a Mixed Bag," *The Gallup Organization* (May 20), www.gallup.com.

Santana, Arthur, and Allan Lengel (2001). "DC Officers Upbraided Over E-Mails," *Washington Post* (March 29), p. B1.

Schevitz, Tanya (2002). "FBI Sees Leap in Anti-Muslim Hate Crimes." *San Francisco Chronicle* (November 26), p. 1.

Schuman, Howard, Charlotte Steeh, Lawrence Bobo, and Maria Krysan (1997). *Racial Attitudes in America.* Cambridge, MA: Harvard University Press.

Selznick, Gertrude J., and Stephen Steinberg (1969). *The Tenacity of Prejudice.* New York: Harper Torchbooks.

Shandley, Robert R. (1998). *Unwilling Germans? The Goldhagen Debate.* Minneapolis: University of Minnesota Press.

Sherif, Muzafer, and Carolyn Sherif (1961). *Intergroup Conflict and Cooperation: The Robbers Cave Experiment.* Norman, OK: University of Oklahoma Press.

Shlachter, Barry (1999). "Jasper Residents Relieved Trial's Over," *Fort Worth Star-Telegram* (February 28), p. 1.

Sidanius, James, Felicia Pratto, and Lawrence Bobo (1994). "Social Dominance Orientation and the Political Psychology of Gender: A Case of Invariance," *Journal of Personality and Social Psychology* 67:998–1011.

Sigall, Harold, and R. Page (1971). "Current Stereotypes: A Little Fading, A Little Faking," *Journal of Personality and Social Psychology* 18:247–255.

Simpson, George E., and J. Milton Yinger (1972). *Racial and Cultural Minorities.* New York: Harper and Row.

Smith, Robert C. (1995). *Racism in the Post Civil Rights Era.* Albany: State University of New York Press.

Sniderman, Paul M., and Thomas Piazza (1993). *The Scar of Race.* Cambridge, MA: The Belknap Press.

Southern Poverty Law Center (2001). "A New Way to Measure America," http://tolerance.org/news/article_tol.jsp?id=140.

——— (2006). "Inspired by Neo-Nazi Tracts, Youth's Rampage Ends in Death," *Intelligence Report* (Spring), p. 4.

Stampp, Kenneth M. (1956). *The Peculiar Institution.* New York: Vintage Books.

Staub, Ervin (1989). *The Roots of Evil: The Origins of Genocide and Other Group Violence.* Cambridge: Cambridge University Press.

Steele, Claude (1992). "Race and the Schooling of Black Americans," *The Atlantic Monthly* (April): 68–78.

————, and J. Aronson (1995). "Stereo-type Threat and the Intellectual Test Performance of African Americans," *Journal of Personality and Social Psychology* 69:797–811.

Steiner, Ivan D., and Homer H. Johnson (1963). "Authoritarianism and Con-formity," *Sociometry* (March): 21–34.

Stephan, W. G. (1986). "The Effects of School Desegregation." In R. Kidd, L. Saxe, and M. Saxe (eds.), *Advances in Applied Social Psychology*. New York: Erlbaum.

Stevick, Eric (2000). "Student Describes Years of Taunting," *Everett Herald* (August 5), p. 1.

Stylinski, Andrzej (2001). "Polish Role Is Admitted in 1941 Massacre," *Boston Globe* (March 16), p. 15.

Sung, Betty Lee (1961). *The Mountain of Gold: The Story of the Chinese in America*. New York: Macmillan.

Tabor, James, and Eugene Gallagher (1995). *Why Waco? Cults and the Battle for Religious Freedom in America*. Berke-ley: University of California Press.

"Taheri-Azar Writes to Eyewitness News," March 14, 2006, www.abc11tv.com. May 2, 2006.

Tajfel, Henri, Michael Billig, R. P. Bundy, and C. Flament (1971). "Social Cate-gorization and Intergroup Behavior," *European Journal of Social Psychology* 1:149–178.

Takagi, Dana Y. (1992). *The Retreat from Race*. New Brunswick, NJ: Rutgers University Press.

Tatum, Beverly Daniel (1997). *"Why Are All the Black Kids Sitting Together in the Cafeteria?"* New York: Basic Books.

Thomas, W. I., and D. S. Thomas (1928). *The Child in America*. New York: Knopf.

Thompson, Cooper, Emmett Schaefer, and Harry Brod (2003). *White Men Chal-lenging Racism: 35 Personal Stories*. Durham: Duke University Press.

Time Magazine (2005). "Survey of a National Adult Hispanics Sample of 503." The Roper Center for Public Opinion Research, University of Con-necticut (July 28–August 3).

Tonry, Michael (1995). *Malign Neglect: Race, Crime, and Punishment in America*. New York: Oxford University Press.

Triandis, Harry C., and Leigh M. Triandis (1972). "Some Studies of Social Dis-tance." In J. Brigham and T. Weiss-bach (eds.), *Racial Attitudes in America*. New York: Harper and Row.

Turner, Patricia A. (1993). *I Heard It Through the Grapevine*. Berkeley: Uni-versity of California Press.

Wachtel, Paul L. (2001). *Race in the Mind of America*. New York: Routledge.

Wall Street Journal (2001). "Sense and the Census" (March 8), p. A22.

Watts, Meredith (1997). *Xenophobia in United Germany*. New York: St. Mar-tin's Press.

Weiss, John (1996). *Ideology of Death: Why the Holocaust Happened in Germany*. Chicago: Ivan R. Dee.

Westie, Frank R. (1964). "Race and Ethnic Relations." In R. E. L. Faris (ed.), *Handbook of Modern Sociology*. Skokie, IL: Rand McNally.

White, Jack E. (1996). "Texaco's High-Octane Racism Problems," *Time* (November 25), p. 23.

———— (1999). "Prejudice? Perish the Thought," *Time* (March 8), p. 36.

Whitmore, Brian (2001). "Bosnia Refugee a Hero to Czech Gypsies," *Boston Globe* (April 1), p. A9.

Wiesel, Elie (1977). "Freedom of Con-science: A Jewish Commentary," *Journal of Ecumenical Studies* 14: 638–649.

Wilhelm, Sidney M. (1970). *Who Needs the Negro?* Cambridge, MA: Schenkman.

Willie, Charles V. (1996). "Dominant and Subdominant People of Power: A New Way of Conceptualizing Minor-ity and Majority Populations," *Sociological Forum* 11(1): 135–152.

Wilson, James Q. (1992). "Crime, Race, and Values," *Society* 91 (November/ December): 90–93.

Word, Carl, Mark Zanna, and Joel Cooper (1974). "The Nonverbal Mediation of Self-Fulfilling Prophecies in Interra-cial Interaction," *Journal of Experimen-tal Social Psychology* 10:109–120.

Wood, Daniel B. (2001). "As Their Numbers Rise, So Does Political Pull," *Christian Science Monitor* (March 16), p. 3.

Woodward, C. Vann (1955). *The Strange Career of Jim Crow.* New York: Oxford University Press.

Wyer, Robert S. Jr., and Thomas K. Srull (1994). *Handbook of Social Cognition.* Hillsdale, NJ: Erlbaum.

Zimbardo, Philip C., Craig Haney, and William C. Banks (1973). "A Pirandellian Prison," *New York Times Magazine* (April 8), p. 7.